TRAPPINGS

TRAPPINGS

STORIES OF

WOMEN, POWER

AND CLOTHING

TWO GIRLS WORKING

Tiffany Ludwig + Renee Piechocki

RUTGERS UNIVERSITY PRESS NEW BRUNSWICK, NEW JERSEY, AND LONDON

Library of Congress Cataloging-in-Publication Data

Ludwig, Tiffany.

Trappings : stories of women, power, and clothing / Two Girls Working: Tiffany Ludwig and Renee Piechocki.

p. cm.

Includes bibliographical references and index.

ISBN 978–0–8135–4184–6 (hardcover : alk. paper)

1. Women—United States—Social conditions. 2. Power (Social sciences)—United States. 3. Women's cloth-ing—United States. 4. Women—United States—Interviews. I. Piechocki, Renee. II. Title.

HQ1421.L83 2007

305.420973'090511—dc22

2007000032

A British Cataloging-in-Publication record for this book is available from the British Library.

Visit our Web site: http://rutgerspress.rutgers.edu

Manufactured in Canada

TEXT DESIGN AND COMPOSITION BY JENNY DOSSIN

TO THE FAMILIES WE CREATE

CONTENTS

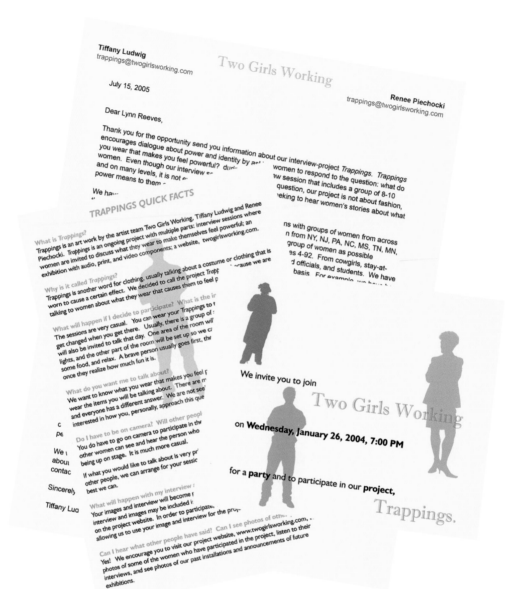

Tiffany Ludwig
trappings@twogirlsworking.com

Two Girls Working

Renee Piechocki
trappings@twogirlsworking.com

July 15, 2005

Dear Lynn Reeves,

Thank you for the opportunity send you information about our interview-project *Trappings*. *Trappings* encourages dialogue about power and identity by a... ... women to respond to the question: what do you wear that makes you feel powerful? ... duri... ... w session that includes a group of 8-10 women. Even though our interview s... ... question, our project is not about fashion, and on many levels, it is not e... ... eking to hear women's stories about what power means to them ...

We ha...

TRAPPINGS QUICK FACTS

What is Trappings?
Trappings is an art work by the artist team Two Girls Working, Tiffany Ludwig and Renee Piechocki. *Trappings* is an ongoing project with multiple parts: interview sessions where women are invited to discuss what they wear to make themselves feel powerful; an exhibition with audio, print, and video components; a website, twogirlsworking.com.

Why is it called Trappings?
Trappings is another word for clothing, usually talking about a costume or clothing that is worn to cause a certain effect. We decided to call the project *Trapp...* ... ...ause we are talking to women about what they wear that causes them to feel p...

What will happen if I decide to participate? What is the i...
The sessions are very casual. You can wear your *Trappings* to t... ... get changed when you get there. Usually, there is a group of ... ... will also be invited to talk that day. One area of the room will ... ... lights, and the other part of the room will be set up so we c... ... some food, and relax. A brave person usually goes first, th... ... once they realize how much fun it is.

What do you want me to talk about?
We want to know what you wear that makes you feel p... ... wear the items you will be talking about. There are m... ... and everyone has a different answer. We are not see... ... interested in how you, personally, approach this que...

Do I have to be on camera? Will other peopl... ...
You do have to go on camera to participate in th... ... other women can see and hear the person who... ... being up on stage. It is much more casual.

If what you would like to talk about is very pr... ... other people, we can arrange for your sessic... ... best we can.

What will happen with my interview ...
Your images and interview will become ... interview and images may be included i... on the project website. In order to participate, ... allowing us to use your image and interview for the proj...

Can I hear what other people have said? Can I see photos of oth... ...
Yes! We encourage you to visit our project website, www.twogirlsworking.com, ... photos of some of the women who have participated in the project, listen to their interviews, and see photos of our past installations and announcements of future exhibitions.

... ns with groups of women from across ... n from NY, NJ, PA, NC, MS, TN, MN, ... group of women as possible ... es 4-92. From cowgirls, stay-at- ... d officials, and students. We have ... basis. For example, ...

We invite you to join

Two Girls Working

on **Wednesday, January 26, 2004, 7:00 PM**

for a **party** and to participate in our **project**,

Trappings.

Interview session invitations, letters, and facts

PREFACE

Trappings is a project by the collaboration Two Girls Working. Between November 2001 and May 2006, we traveled across the United States gathering groups of women together to respond to the question *What do you wear that makes you feel powerful?*

Our collaboration was born out of being compelled to work together. We met in February 2000 while working on a conference in Brooklyn, New York. Sensing that greater things were possible, we vowed to keep in touch when Renee moved to North Carolina, ending the first and last time we ever lived within an hour of each other.

We knew each other as colleagues, but did not know each other as artists. We spent the rest of 2000 learning about each other's work, e-mailing images of our artwork and speaking about our backgrounds and what inspired our artistic practices. There were common denominators: dedication to creating work outside of the studio, engagement with new audiences, and curiosity about the fact that some of our friends were rejecting the word *feminism*, even though those same friends acknowledged wanting all that feminism had to offer: equal pay, equal opportunities, and infinite possibilities. We sensed a dearth of feminist projects operating outside of the framework of universities and large cities. *Trappings* and the question *What do you wear that makes you feel powerful?* grew out of this scenario.

Interview sessions are the heart of our project. The first was held in Jersey City, New Jersey, in November 2001. To create the interview sessions, we purposefully appropriate a format familiar to many women: the house party (think Mary Kay or Tupperware or sex toys). We work to find a host, and ask her to gather a group of friends, neighbors, and colleagues to participate. They have been held just about anyplace, including homes, offices, classrooms, places of worship, and community spaces. All of the participants are given an invitation that explains what will happen at the session. When they arrive, there is food and drink and time to mingle. We give a brief description about the project and answer questions.

This is where *Trappings* takes its own direction. We are not asking women to buy lipstick, a plastic container to hold lipstick, or a vibrator that looks like a lipstick. In fact, they don't have to buy anything. We are asking them to discuss what power means and how they identify with power through clothing. One at a time, each woman steps into an area of the room that has been designated as a stage. She is miked, the lights turn on, and the cameras roll. While the other women who are attending the session watch, she is asked to introduce herself and respond to the project question. The interview session is recorded on a series of digital video and still cameras.

We did not set out to meet 536 women in fifteen states. When the project began, we saw one week of interviews and one exhibition. But once that week was over, we knew it would continue. Sixty-six *Trappings* interview sessions later, we have met with women in each region of the United States. We have interviewed women in New Jersey, New York, Mississippi, Tennessee, North Carolina, Washington, Minnesota, Wyoming, Montana, Pennsylvania, Michigan, Missouri, Alaska, New Mexico, and Massachusetts.

A wide range of women have come to *Trappings* interview sessions, from

Interview session stills

diesel engineers, stay-at-home mothers, and community volunteers to fashion-industry executives, artists, and elected officials. In addition to sessions hosted by individuals, we have been invited to produce interview sessions for organizations such as a quilting circle, an after-school group for at-risk teenage women, a drag-king performance group, YWCAs, museums, a chapter of Dress for Success, a university mentor program, and women's centers. We have worked to produce interview sessions that encourage diversity in terms of ethnicity, class, education, cultural heritage, age, and geography.

Trappings strives to present the women in their own voices. The texts in this book are edited excerpts from their transcribed interviews. At times, we have edited for length, including only one or two of the main themes that women presented in their interviews. At other times, we have edited for continuity, placing texts about similar themes together to aid readability. We have edited very, very sparingly for content and grammar; the texts are the women speaking to you in their own voices in their own way.

We have taken the same approach to our photographs. The images are of women as they appeared at their interview sessions. We have worked with the

Interview session stills

images to dramatize the background, but have not "enhanced" the women's portraits. Their interviews reflect a brief moment of their lives caught on film. If we had met them one month earlier, or later, the answers from some of our participants might have been different. To help present a more three-dimensional view of the stories, we have asked some women to send us their own photographs of events, places, or people in their lives. In some cases, we included short facts that relate to the interviews. We also revisited a few of our participants, to capture images and further the stories they presented in their interview sessions.

Trappings has evolved into a project with multiple parts, including the interview sessions; an archive of participants' audio interviews and portraits; exhibitions in museums, galleries, and public places; and now this book. The book contains portraits and stories of sixty-one women. We hope that you are inspired to encounter the other women who participated in this project on our Web site, www.TwoGirlsWorking.com.

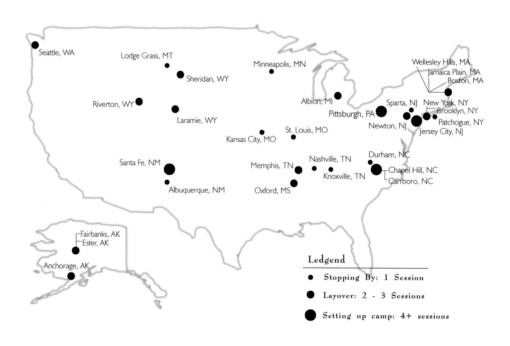

Trappings Interview Locations 2001–2006

ACKNOWLEDGMENTS

Trappings is a collaborative project on many levels. This project would not exist if women did not want to be interviewed. We would like to thank everyone who attended an interview session, and especially the session hosts who opened their worlds to us. Portraits and a list of all participants appear at the end of this book. We would like to especially thank the people who helped make the road feel like home by offering us places to stay, home-cooked meals, and sometimes wine at five o'clock: Connie and Kerry Ozer, Carissa Hussong, Alicia Faxon, Elizabeth D.M. Wise and Glenn Haase, Kathi and Mike Miller, Barbara Goldstein and John Pastier, Tracey and Ed Acevedo, Sandi Gillespie, Susan Olson and Lauren Miller, Leah Hardy and Mark Ritchie, and Dorothy Crabb.

Our process includes creating a transcription of each woman's interview. We would like to thank all of our transcribers who have helped us with the tedious and essential task, especially Vicki Bell, Dee Dee Connell, Sara Donatelli, Donna Edwards, Phyllis Flint, Veronica Harris, Anna Marie Ludwig, Lynn Reeves, and Kelly Rutan. We thank Molly Blieden for encouraging us from the beginning to have all of the interviews transcribed. We forgive Heidi Card for her efforts at transcribing, but thank her for her research assistance with this book.

Trappings interview sessions have been funded by a mix of public, private, and personal pockets. We would like to thank the individuals who contributed to our interview session fund: Cathie Behrend, Charlotte Cohen, Wendy Feuer, Phyllis and Rob Flint, Abigail Flynn-Kozara and David Kozara, Paula Gilhooley, Ellen Golden, Kim Hafner, Elizabeth Theobald Irvin and Will Irvin, Regina Piechocki Kiser and Bob Kiser, Elfie Knecht, Lorri and Jeff Mac Harg, Joyce Marus-Sullivan, Laura Jean McDermott-Camp and John Camp, Jennifer McGregor, Guy Nordenson, Clare Norrins, Celia O'Donnell and Edwin Torres, Susan Olson and Lauren Miller, Jennifer and Steven Schell Podoll, Mary L. Pretz-Lawson, Jen Sale and Luke Miller, AnnMarie and Orlando Santiago, Amy Schichtel, Amy Sedlazek, Shannon Flattery Sharp and Jonathan Sharp, Chriss Slevin, Karen and Peter Slotta, Harley Spiller, Dr. Sheilagh Weymouth, Elizabeth D.M. Wise and Glenn Haase, Judith and Stanley Zabar, and Sigurlaug and

William Zetwick. We also thank the following organizations that funded interview sessions: Orange County Arts Commission, the Financial Women's Association's mentor program at Baruch College, Mid-Atlantic Arts Foundation's Artists & Communities program, Greater Pittsburgh Arts Council's PA Partners in the Arts program, the Sprout Fund's Seed Award program, The Pittsburgh Foundation, the National Endowment for the Arts, The Heinz Endowments, Central Wyoming College, Albion College, the University of Wyoming, Simmons College, and Washington University in St. Louis. We also thank the New York Foundation for the Arts' Fiscal Sponsorship Program.

On the road again, unloading after a cross-country trip

Since we do not live in the same state, studio time together is very valuable. While we spend a lot of time visiting each other, we greatly appreciate the places that have given us a location to work and inspiring environments: Jentel Artist Residency Program, Virginia Center for the Creative Arts, and Santa Fe Art Institute.

We would like to thank our friends and families for their support, encouragement, and understanding when we had to miss opportunities to get together because we were on the road or under a tough deadline. Most importantly, we would like to thank Ryan Hughes and Rob Owen for helping us find emergency software, for building crates, for not batting an eye when we disappear for six weeks, and for trusting us when we say, "We've got a great idea."

INTRODUCTION

If you received an invitation from your mother, a colleague, your best friend, or a neighbor to come to a party where you would be interviewed, on camera, in a group of ten other women, and asked to respond to the question *What do you wear that makes you feel powerful?* how would you respond? Would you respond at all or would you shy away, claiming other obligations? Would you agree to attend, knowing there is safety in numbers? Would you try on a dozen outfits and bring six of them with you to illustrate the complicated nature of power in your life? Or do you know immediately what your single power source is?

Before you delve into the images and stories contained in this book, you might want to consider the clothes hanging in your closet. If there is an article of clothing that makes you feel powerful, go ahead and put it on—wear it while you read this book. If your power is not revealed through clothing, have an idea of what power means to you and how you express it; this will put you in the same position as the sixty-one women presented in the pages ahead.

Trappings would not exist if no one came to the party. Luckily, everywhere we visited, women were ready to claim the stage and really ready to listen to stories that other women had to share. There is no script. There is only one question. Women choose what they want to reveal or what their friends or colleagues coax them into discussing.

This project is not about fashion and to a large extent not even about clothing. From the start, we knew that we wanted to speak with a diverse range of women about topics they may not have considered before. We wanted to speak with them about feminism. We wanted to speak with them about the cultural constraints of female identity. We wanted to speak with them about the role of power in their lives and what made them powerful. But we knew that if we only focused on power and the f-word, either no one would come to our party or we might not get beyond black-and-white answers and into real stories of women's lives. The women we met have given us answers we did not know existed. Clothing is the common denominator; clothing is something everyone has a relationship with. You can manipulate it as a vehicle for self-expression or you can avoid it altogether. Everyone gets dressed. Our identification of clothing as an outward projection of personality, class, occupation, and lifestyle, as well as personal history, memory, and identity led to our project question. By asking women *What do you wear that makes you feel powerful?* we ask them to consider what power means to them and how it is they turn it on.

From the beginning, we have been determined not to present a right answer or develop a thesis. We do not want to create a Super Power Girl, a composite of the women we have met: a hockey-playing English teacher with a law degree who wears one flat shoe and one stiletto despite the fact that she feels most powerful when she's in her comfortable jeans doing community service with her best friends after her morning twenty-mile run for a good cause. Super Power Girl would represent the most common answers at the cost of the layered stories of individuals.

There is no right answer. That is not a sidestep in the face of a difficult question. After the first interview sessions, and after developing exhibitions about the work, we became aware that our project also provides viewers with the opportunity to examine judgments or assumptions they make based on appearance. We have been the project creators, but also project viewers. After meeting more than five hundred women, across the United States, in all sorts of situations, we have developed a wider lens of understanding. We want the women in this book to give you the same opportunity. We hope that the person you think you will love makes you crazy, and that you see parts of your own story in someone whose friendship you have not yet sought.

Not just a project where two nice girls set up lunch and get together to chitchat with girlfriends and take some photos, this is an artwork that causes people to think, a project with a social framework. At a time when women's rights are being challenged in the United States and the status of women around the world is still second class at best, we want to inspire women to become empowered in their own lives.

THE STORIES

Linda Durham

Santa Fe, New Mexico | July 2005

I think of myself as a risk-taker. I think other people think of me as a gallery owner. The word that comes to mind when I think of power is *access,* and access to me means a whole lot of things: access to information, access to people, access to ideas. So I'm, in a way, an access freak. There are certain phrases that stick with me. They're kind of modern mantras. And one of them is "Pay Attention." That's something I attempt to do all the time, to pay attention to where I am, and to what I'm doing, and to what opportunities are available to me.

I was thinking about *What do I wear that would make me feel powerful?* Well, I'm sixty-two years old, and I've gone through a lot of incarnations. I got my

Equity card when I was thirteen, and I worked in the theater, and my dream was always to move to New York. I got to New York in 1965. It was during a big newspaper strike. I was pretty naïve. I thought I would just look in the newspaper and find a job as an actor, but there were no newspapers, so I went to an employment agency. One agent said, "Well, they're casting for Playboy bunnies." I didn't even know what that was. But the casting call was like a theatrical casting call. We had to wear little bathing suits and leotards. And I got to change my name, so I felt like I had a character and a costume. I could make up stories about myself because we weren't really permitted to tell our last names or where we lived. It was very powerful.

A lot of people at that time thought Playboy was demeaning to women. But it never seemed like that to me. We made lots of money. When I was nineteen years old, I was making more money than my father made to raise a family of five. I met all kinds of people, and it opened the world to me. It was a great time. Playboy was not a phenomenon that traveled well into the seventies. To me, it was a thing of the sixties and you had to be there.

I learned that men want you to like them, you know, that they're afraid of you. Later on in business, that gave me an edge because when I went to a bank, a very male-dominated business at that time, to borrow money, I knew those bankers and I knew that they were nervous, and I understood what their jobs were. And I understood what my motive was. *I want money. You are a person who lends money as your job. You will lend the money to me.*

There were lots of times when to feel powerful all I had to do was wear something that was formfitting, when your physical presence, especially if you came out of that Playboy pseudo-glamorous world, gave you enough power. It gave me an opportunity to learn about the kind

Trappings interview portrait,
Linda Durham Contemporary Art Gallery

of power that many women outgrow, and I think I'm outgrowing it: power over men or in those sexual situations. You can have access by being a beautiful, sexy, young woman. Something that I think of now in this age is *How do I continue to have power and feel valid when I'm not in that category?* It's very possible to do—curiosity about other people, interest in other people.

In my pocket, there's the accessory that I always have with me. It makes me feel secure and powerful. It's my passport. And it does have a Russian passport cover on it, which has gotten me into a little bit of trouble in some of the countries I've visited. I've visited sixty-four countries, and I like to look through it to see some of the places I've been. In my risk-taking life I've climbed Mount Kilimanjaro, all 19,341 feet of it. And I've gone to wild islands and faraway places. And Baghdad in 2004. I was in Haiti six months ago. My favorite place is Burma. But of all the places I've gone, it's the markets and the schools and the parks and the people that I like to experience. I traveled alone most of the time, and in traveling alone in a foreign country where the culture is not that familiar and the language is unknown, there's a sense of learning *Who am I?* Who am I when my popularity as a gallery owner or the people who know me are stripped away? Am I a person who loves other people and who appreciates the opportunity to be with them? And maybe the passport represents that to me.

And there's one more thing. It starts way back when I first moved to New Mexico in 1966. I had just left the city, New York, and moved to the desert, to several hundred acres. My new husband and I were building our own house and living without electricity, without a telephone, without running water. And my first spring in the desert one windy day, a windy day like only could happen in New Mexico, I went out for a hike by myself. I climbed up into the sandstone rocks, and the wind was blowing and the dust was swirling and I stood at the edge of the cliff and I said, "God, please tell me, am I here for a reason? Does it mean anything? I need a sign. I'm lonely, I'm out of place, please give me a sign." And just then, two ravens flew out from behind me and hung in the wind over the edge of the cliff in front of me. To me that was a sign that you have a purpose. That it's okay, that things will unfold, that there's order, that there's opportunity, that there's adventure, that there's flight. I made up a whole language for them, what messages they were bringing me if there were three of them, if they flew in front of my car, if they were on a stop sign.

Two years ago I decided to do something very powerful, and that was to have ravens on my shoulder. So that's my power, and I wear it and hardly anyone sees it.

Erika Mann

Chapel Hill, North Carolina | April 2003

Trappings interview portrait,
Women's Center

The reason I chose what I'm wearing today is because it makes me feel very powerful as a sixteen-year-old in high school. It makes me feel so much more comfortable when I have this on.

A lot of times I wrap my hair when I have nothing else to do with it, but I chose to wrap my hair today in kente cloth because it's my way of feeling good about who I am. I am very uncomfortable with my body, so wearing these things are like my comfort zone. It took me a very long time as an American to find out who I am as a person. Finding out who I am as a person through history, ancestors, and where I came from gave me a lot more pride, as in who I am as a person and as an individual.

It started when I was in the sixth grade. I had a lot of problems with teachers making racial comments towards me and telling me that I couldn't make it. I didn't know how to deal with it. When I switched schools, there was this lady named Miss Scott. And Miss Scott was a history teacher, the first African American history teacher I've ever had. She told me that I should be proud of who I am. She noticed during the summertime I will always wear a coat, because I have this thing with my arms and being a big person. She would teach me other things, like about my heritage. I became more comfortable with who I was as a person, and I had a lot more pride. She's a very inspirational person in my life.

Sometimes kids at school are cruel, even those who are of the same culture as myself. Females, males. Like, "Why you wear that?" or "Why did you decide to put that on this morning? That doesn't make any sense." Or some of the Caucasian students in my class will think: "I think that's a little too bold. Why are you doing that? Are you doing it just to stand out as an African American? Are you doing that to poke fun at people?" And then I have to explain to them, no, this is just me, this is who I am as an individual, not just as an African American.

I have two African natives who live right next door to me. They're from Sierra Leone and I've seen them in a couple of things that I really like. They interest me a lot. They've had bad situations with other African American kids who pick on their way of speaking. When you think about it, that's everyone. No matter what you do in life, there's always going to be someone there to critique you on how you are, what you look like, or how you dress, or the way you speak.

Kente cloth originated in Ghana in the twelfth century. This strip-woven cloth was historically the cloth of kings. Today, its use is widespread and international. Wearing kente cloth is comparable to wearing an evening gown or tuxedo in Western culture.

I'm with Urban Leaders of Tomorrow. Great organization. I'm chairperson. But it's not a women's organization. It just so happens that a lot of girls come, so we do a lot of girl things. Like yesterday we did nail art, which we got really excited about. I love nail art. We all love nail art. We've done a potluck, which was very successful. We're gonna do a mother-daughter day. We're gonna have like a spa, do nails, and facials, and massages, and have a lot of fun. Try to like establish more bonding between the mothers and the daughters of the community.

I'm a very outspoken person. I've done a lot of things in my life that I have no shame of. I speak out against whatever I think is wrong. I want to become a lawyer-slash-businessperson. I'll probably be in and out of college for the rest of my life. But in ten years, I'll have lots of money. That's my goal, and to help my family, and to buy my mom a house, and to give back to my community, as well as the schools I was in. To be honest, I just want to help as many people as possible. That makes me very happy, to be able to help other people.

I am attending A+T State University. I'm out here on my own. It's not easy; it's not fun. I've met some college students whose parents are always with them, and they don't understand responsibility. For a while I was upset with those people because it was kind of like *Why is it that people who have everything are like as if they are continuously blessed?* And I who have nothing come here and I fight all of my life. But then you have to realize in the end, you going to get your blessing, too.

A lot of us go there and we don't have families who can financially support us. I hold down two jobs. When you think about it, seven dollars an hour, you are probably working twenty hours, you're not going to get but almost a hundred dollars. And you still can't pay your rent. My landlord is African American—it's not like he tries to help. I really want people to know, especially black people, if you see someone struggling and they're in school: help them.

For instance, I walk up and down the street all day. To the bus stop, walk to the store, whatever I'm doing. I don't have a car. And it upsets me that people, especially African Americans who have cars, don't stop and say, Honey, you need help with those twenty grocery bags you carryin'? And when they do stop they're trying to hit on me. It's real aggravating. But you find that everybody's

not like that. They're really some good people out there. And I've had some, a lot of help.

Now feeling powerful, it's still in the clothes I wear. But now power is within yourself and being honest and true as much as possible. Power to me is the ability to adapt to any situation and go through things and say, you know what? I'm still gonna kick butt tomorrow. I don't want to be anybody's baby mama. I refuse to be stuck out here in the world on my own with a baby. Trying to raise this child and still looking for love myself? That's ridiculous. You can get a government check but you won't have a life. My goal is to do the best I can. I want to be wealthy. I want to show the world how to do this the right way.

Claire A. Yannacone

Patchogue, New York | December 2001

I'm wearing engineer-y clothes 'cause I've been working as an engineer on a ship for like the last five years. It kind of feels good to wear steel toe-cap boots and have a bunch of tools in your back pocket. There's something inherently powerful about that.

On the ship I worked on, there were four engines. There was a big main engine, a 690 horsepower from 1965. If you took a Cadillac and put it on its side and stuck it in a room, that would be the size of this engine. So you deal with the engines, you deal with all of the electrical systems for the boat, you deal with all the plumbing. If it's mechanical it's your responsibility, more or less. It's a lot of maintenance. Whenever everything is going fine nobody notices that it's all working, but as soon as, like, the head doesn't flush, or the light doesn't go on, it's like a crisis.

In New York harbor, I only know of five women that work on tugboats. One's a captain, one's a mate. I don't know of any engineers. I don't know if it's like the Old Boys Network. A lot of women probably think it requires an extraordinary amount of strength, which it doesn't. Once you are working on very big engines, nobody can lift the head. Women have a better sense of, *Well, okay, I'm not going to pick that up, so I'd better get a chain fall from here to there, and a line.* You can do the same thing, you just have to think instead of just—*ugh, ugh, move thing.* You just do more thinking.

Dirty girl at work

We were in South Africa, and we had a whole lot of engine work to do, and it was in the bearings, in the lower part of the engine, and it was really oily and incredibly dirty. You are lying on your back, on the floor, and you got your hands in the engine and all that. We were docked at Victoria and Albert Mall in Capetown. So you think, *God, I'm working all day, I want an ice cream.* And you're in your coveralls and you're like, *Well, I'm gonna go get an ice cream.* And you go like striding into the mall, and the waters part, you know, and people just go, There's that dirty girl. They're not used to it and they don't know what to make of it, but there's something powerful about it. You're like, *Yeah, I work with my hands, I work with my body, I'm dirty, what's it to you?* It's different, and I guess that's why it's powerful. It's also not expected, which is nice.

All of the women on the ship, all of the women that I hung out with, more specifically, were similar to me. We all were strong and kind of dirty and had nasty clothes, but you know, the patches we'd put on them ourselves, and I think we all had that same powerful ideal. When we did

Picton Castle
under full sail

put on our street clothes and go ashore, we'd still have this swagger of, *I'm tougher than you. I do cool things.* And you were just waiting for someone to ask, "What do you do?" *I work on a square-rigger. I can kick your ass and I know it.* And that power went through the whole ship.

You know what was the funniest? They were so used to seeing me every day in really disgusting clothing, when I got dressed up to go out, that was a whole different kind of powerful thing. Because then they'd be, "Whoa, you are a woman. Oh my God, who could tell?" You never quite knew how to take that.

Trappings interview portrait,
Piechocki family home

Mary Turner Lane

I grew up in a very conventional childhood. Learned all of the things and did all of the things that good little girls do. Went to college because that was expected of me. Came out with an English major and a teacher's certificate, which would certainly carry you in that world until you married. And when you married it was clear that a husband would take care of you. That was guaranteed almost. So I did exactly that and went through World War II, and then lo and behold, to my great surprise, I was a widow. I was twenty-nine years old with a two-year-old child.

So there I was. I could teach school for the rest of my life, but I really didn't want to do that. It took me about five years to get over grief and stress and decide that I had to do something. I had very good friends that encouraged me to come to Chapel Hill. I did, and I got a master's in education with a focus on English. I was asked to stay on at the university for a dollar an hour and work with the teacher education program as an instructor, which is certainly the lowest financial classification in which you can find yourself. Interestingly enough, it became the classification for one hundred women. I knew I had to get a doctorate.

In 1970, we had worked for civil rights, and it was time to work for women's rights. I worked so hard in

Trappings interview portrait,
Jean Parrish's home

9

trying to pass the ERA. I was active in student affairs on campus. I had a student come to me and say, "Oh, we want to bring Phyllis Schlafly to campus." I said, "You can't do that unless you have Betty Friedan at the same time." So we had a debate between Phyllis Schlafly and Betty Friedan.

I had about five friends in the College of Arts and Sciences. We were sort of the troublemakers, I guess. We met every week because things were getting bad for the few faculty women that were here. We had a lot of horror stories going on. So we researched the possibility of a women's studies program. And we found out, yes, that's coming into being. We had the framework for it; we already had an interdisciplinary degree in which women's studies would fit. So the faculty council passed it, and then the chancellor said that the director had to come from this campus. We thought we could bring in a star. But we didn't get a star. We got me.

I didn't know what a risk-taker I was until I decided to take that job. I knew that the first two years had to be teaching the faculty, 80 percent male, what women's studies was all about. So that's what I took on. The chancellor encouraged me, and the dean of the College of Arts and Sciences encouraged me. I got questions from the men: "Now, what is women's studies? Why don't we have men's studies?" And I said just as carefully and precisely, "Because that's all we've ever had is men's studies. You never learned anything about women except about Joan of Arc and Queen Elizabeth, did you?" And the men said, "No, we really didn't."

We had a series of seminars that first year. The fourth lecturer was Margaret Mead, who was very popular with women at that time. Well, that night I had a sort of epiphany. We held this lecture in Memorial Hall. I introduced the program and then had a member of our board introduce Margaret Mead. I had been to many lectures in Memorial Hall, and I realized that this was the first time I had seen all women control the stage. We were in charge of the stage. We were in charge of the program. We were somebody!

I must confess that what I wore that night was designated to make a statement. Clothes can carry a stamp of authority and approval. I do think as a woman, you serve as a role model in a variety of ways. So clothes were simply a part of what I did. You not only taught on campus, you went off campus to many places to lecture, to speak, to represent the University of North Carolina, to represent women's studies. You joined organizations, and again you were a representative of something. So clothes became important to me.

This outfit is a statement. Once I bought this outfit, I could go anywhere to speak. I was sure of that. Visually it's good. Stylistically it's good. I think I've been wearing this outfit fifteen years, and I feel just as good in it now as I did then.

Memorial Hall: site of Mary Turner's epiphany

"Equality of rights under the law shall not be denied or abridged by the United States or by any state on account of sex."

You may be shocked to know that this is not included in the United States Constitution. It would be if the Equal Rights Amendment (ERA), written by Alice Paul and first introduced into Congress in 1923, had been ratified.

When Congress finally passed it and submitted it to the states for ratification in 1972, even legions of women as tough as Mary Turner Lane couldn't make it happen. Only thirty-five states (of the necessary thirty-eight) have ratified it. The fifteen states that have not are Alabama, Arizona, Arkansas, Florida, Georgia, Illinois, Louisiana, Mississippi, Missouri, Nevada, North Carolina, Oklahoma, South Carolina, Utah, and Virginia.

La'Tasha D. Mayes

Pittsburgh, Pennsylvania | January 2005

I've been living in Pittsburgh for six years now. I'm a master's student at Carnegie Mellon in the Heinz School for public policy, and I happen to be studying reproductive health policy. I can start by talking about my outfit.

One thing I wear all the time is my ankh. It represents the key to eternal life for the pharaohs, it also represents a man and a woman coming together to create life, also the universal force or God. I wear that every day. First I started off wearing a little ankh, but they just kept getting bigger and bigger. So this is the latest installment, but eventually I have to get like an iced-out ankh with diamonds so I have some bling bling. But the other thing that I wear every single day is this ring. I realize it's almost sort of a symbolic protection for me. I think of myself as being very independent, and I don't happen to drive, so when I'm on a bus late at night I don't walk around with fear, at least in terms of somebody invading my personal space.

And the hat that I have on now is a hat that I've been waiting for all my life, actually. This hat says, "You sharp." I mean, that's the type of disposition I always want people to have of me because I am sharp. I know I'm intelligent, I know how to articulate what I think, what I feel—well, most of the time. I don't want to give the appearance that I have it together, I want people to know that I do have it together, and it's not just something I do, it's just something I am.

I have my power outfit, this is the foundation of it, but I mean when I put on this next piece, people know that I'm going for the power thing, okay? So I'm going to get that. I love, I love this jacket. I was going through a lot of changes at the point where I actually purchased the coat. My mom purchased it, in all reality. Every time I wore it, people would start to say to me, "Tasha, you look really nice today" or "That's a sharp coat." I know it wasn't the coat so much as I guess my disposition walking around with this coat on. When I put on this coat it almost enhances the sum total of who I am. I'll be very honest, it's also very radical looking. I've been told I have like a radical look because, I mean, I am a black woman, but I decided to cut off my permed hair. At the same time, I'm wearing my ankh and saying radical things. The coat only added to that image.

The most memorable experience I've had with this coat is the day that I met Angela Davis. See now, I didn't know I was going to tell this story. I will never forget planning for her to be at the University of Pittsburgh, where I went undergrad. She was talking about globalism, terrorism, and gender. We were in David Lawrence auditorium and everybody was there, the walls were lined with people. It was like, it was like Jesus arriving in Nazareth or some-

thing, and I remember I was the one walking with her down the aisle to give her lecture. I felt so powerful walking with her, but additionally had my coat on.

I'll never forget being introduced as a person on campus who repre-sented the black community at the University of Pittsburgh, but also as the person who represented the women's community, and at that time the feminist community on campus. I was starting to become a black femi-nist on campus. Radical black feminist on campus with her radical leather jacket introducing a radical person from our herstory. So I'm introduced, and it's like six hundred, seven hun-dred people in this auditorium. I read this two-paragraph speech and there was not a noise in the crowd, and I in-troduced her and I sat down. And when she walked by me she was like, you know, "Thank you." The first thing she said was not "I'm Angela Davis" or "Let me begin my talk." She said, "I could of have sat there and lis-tened to La'Tasha continue to talk." For me that was powerful. That is probably my most memorable experi-

Trappings interview portrait,
Cecile Springer's home

ence with my coat, at that juncture when I was calling myself a feminist. Because I'm not anymore.

Many women of my generation, when they got to college, it was the first time that they could articulate the oppression that they felt. I felt the same way. I was the quintessential feminist, and I subscribed to all the tenets of feminism for about a year and a half, only looking at gender as a form of oppression. I was really entrenched in this feminism thing, I mean rah-rahing in the streets, the whole thing. I was the vice president of the feminist organization on campus. There had never been black women in the organization, but also never in a leadership position such as that. And so really, that was kind of a motivation for other women of color to join. And one day, one of the really radical black males in the black organization, he said, "Oh, who is La'Tasha? Is that that black girl in that white women's organization?" I was livid because for the first time I recognized I had only been looking at my identity through sex and gender, and it kind of hurt me deeply because I didn't know I was doing that. I got caught up in feminism and I felt like at that moment, that was when I was betrayed by feminism. Because it didn't prepare me. We didn't talk about race. We didn't talk about class, we didn't talk about sexual orientation, we didn't talk about ability or any of those things. I still subscribe to the tenets of feminism. I remember distinctly going from this predominately women's feminist organization to the black organization. The difference was I took the gender lens with me to that black organization, and that made the biggest difference for me. My problem with white women in particular and feminism is that they don't recognize that their experience is not universal. And so that's why women of color, in my opinion, and black women in particular, shy away from feminism or something called black feminism. I'm not a derivative. I am something totally different, and feminism does not capture that for me, and I know it doesn't capture the experience of women of color and black women in that terminology.

Power, I believe, it's the accumulation of influence to achieve a desired outcome. I used to always want to be excellent, but I remember a lecturer saying many steps beyond that is being significant. So, for me, I think that that drives my idea of power, and the idea of having power *over* someone is totally different than having power *with* someone. We can talk about inherited power. But women in this country, and black people in this country, they didn't all have money to bring about significant systemic changes. And it's almost like universal power. It's a force that's within you. Some people will call it divine or spiritual, but that's the type of power or influence I want to work with. Not those trappings of being earthly or in the world, but working on the spiritual component. Sometimes you don't have control of the type of power that you do have, and sometimes we don't recognize the significance or magnitude of power *with* that we have.

Pittsburgh, Pennsylvania | September 2006

We all change. I really don't wear those things anymore. I lost my ring, which was devastating. I still have the jacket. I used to wear it every day, but now I don't. I still wear it to convey power. My ankh, I have supersized it. It is like eight times bigger than before. I wear it all the time and I wear it in different places, kinda to see how people react to it. Or how they interact with it.

I can't wear hats anymore really, because my hair has grown. I still think about how people reacted to me in the hat, compared to how they react to me with my hair now. Hair is an interesting thing, especially amongst black women. We just have this very complex relationship with our hair. At the time of the last taping, I had just started to lock my hair, and it was a process. People always say you have to be ready to lock your hair. Because it's not only a commitment and a lesson in patience, but also it represents a spiritual connection to the universe, or your higher power, or what have you. I'm very proud of my hair, and I don't think I feel like I have to wear hats or need to wear hats anymore.

My hair is very powerful because it defies social convention. Just because I have the hair that I do, just because I have the skin color that I do, those things do not equal who I am, but they just represent who I am. They're symbolic of who I am, and that's a powerful statement, you know? I could decide to cut it all off tomorrow and still be the same person. But the way people judge you based on your appearance, that's the unfortunate part. I want my appearance to represent pride in myself, but also pride in being a woman and being a woman of color, being a black woman, and that I defy social convention. So that's my hair.

This is my power chair. It was given to me in December of 2005 by Vanessa German. This is the first gift that I was ever given where I cried, like, I didn't have anything to say. The instant I saw it I cried. Because, I mean, there's so much to it. That red is a power color for me. The ankh is just representative of who I am. On the seat, I wrote this quote about what inspires me. It says, "I am inspired by the powerfully passionate and indefatigable spirit of women." Who uses that word *indefatigable* besides me? I've maybe sat in it three times, because this is my source of power symbolically, when I'm trying to figure out major things in my life. It's just so powerful that it represents like all the women who have come before, all of the ancestors who have come before. I can go to this place and be renewed and sit in this chair. It's rare, because of how powerful it is to me and what it represents.

Why are we here at Freedom Corner? This was the place where during the civil rights movement, everyone would come here. Before it was just a place, there

La'Tasha at Freedom Corner

was no monument here. This was the launching point for marches, for rallies. Freedom Corner is symbolic of all these people who gave their lives essentially to the work. But for me, it's about black women in particular who have done the work, but weren't recognized for all that they did in order for us to be free. My life's work will be dedicated to social justice, reproductive justice for women of color in particular. Just like my chair, I can come here. These are reservoirs of inspiration.

Colleen Wyse

New York, New York | November 2001

I am the publisher of *Women's Wear Daily,* which is a fashion publication for the fashion and beauty and retail industries. So I work with tons of women, not only at my own place of employment and our own publication, but also women who work in those industries. And it is a very female-dominated industry. There are tons of powerful women.

Power is perhaps different in that way, because I can't say we're not competing with men—we certainly are—but I often have found it fascinating that there are so many women in powerful positions that you take it for granted. *Of course I'm going to the top, there's nothing else.* I remember someone said to me, "The only time women and men are on the equal playing ground is in college, and after that everything else is changed." I don't know that that's actually the case, but I do find it interesting in talking with other women who are perhaps in more male-dominated industries or perhaps a more fifty-fifty split, that they still talk about what I think are old stereotypes. I don't see them anymore. It's expected that women will be the leaders in meetings, it's expected that we will dress the way we want to dress, and we will act the way expected of any powerful person, and quite frankly, you often see women in power not wanting it to be discussed that we're women. I think that's probably more and more the case of many women today. If they are featured in an article about power or

Trappings interview portrait,
Women's Wear Daily office

WHAT AM I BUMPING MY HEAD ON?

The Glass Ceiling: This term was coined in the early 1980s to define the invisible barrier women and minorities faced as they attempted to elevate their positions at work.

The Report: In 1991, Secretary of Labor Elizabeth Dole and her successor Lynn Martin addressed this problem, publicizing it in A Report on the Glass Ceiling Initiative. *This report inspired Title II of the Civil Rights Act of 1991, which established the Glass Ceiling Commission. Its mission was to conduct a study and prepare appropriate recommendations on "eliminating artificial barriers to the advancement of women and minorities . . . to management and decision-making positions in business."*

The Results: When the commission's report was released in 1995, it stated that very few women and minorities were in top positions and that when they did manage to rise to the top, they earned less than white men. The glass ceiling still exists: According to the study Income, Poverty, and Health Insurance Coverage in the United States: 2005, *published by the U.S. Census Bureau, women earned only seventy-seven cents for every dollar earned by a man.*

about leadership, they would prefer that their gender is downplayed rather than overplayed.

Power and dress is a very interesting thing depending on the industry. When you work in the beauty and fashion industry, it is expected that you will be fashionable, but I think more so, you're able to be yourself. I find that most women in this industry dress perhaps less formally than women in other industries because we can do anything. I see women dressing so sexily I've seen them at the beach in the same kind of attire, and even I am somewhat shocked, but what I realize is that it's all about the fashion. It's not about the judgment. It's about the style, and about the look, and it's a ton of fun. That's still a powerful position because you're dressing with style.

I remember starting out in the business, when we were all wearing suits and we wore the little bow ties, and bit by bit things became more and more casual, but not without style. And not without, shall I say, sophistication and seriousness. It's not as though we're wearing business suits any longer. I haven't worn a suit in two, three years. Sweaters, skirts, boots, stocking-less, stockings, sling backs, stilettos are all part of the regular business attire. And casual Fridays have become casual Monday through Fridays. Granted, maybe the power attire is a little different when you have a business client call, but it's perhaps a subtle difference.

I finally had to admit, I think I'm more married to the beauty and fashion category than I care to admit. I felt like that was kind of a coming of age for me. I grew up in the seventies. We were marching, we were, you know, holding it high. I detest people referring to people on their staff as girls. Girls are twelve to fourteen. We grew up on that, we knew that, and so to be able to then realize that the beauty and fashion industry is a legitimate industry, and a very powerful one, was nice, and you could kind of breathe a little more.

When you work with all women, it is the best situation in the world. Those terms, those stereotypes are nonexistent. I've never ever had a negative experience. And maybe it's because the environments I work in are *do your job, get it done, move it on, do it well*. It's difficult to attach any negative stereotype to that situation. Really, at most any magazine—I was at *W*, there's no glass ceiling, there are all women at the top. *Glamour*, absolutely the same. But the further back I go in years, the more men who were in the business and at the top, it was more the norm. Now it can be and it can't be, but you don't feel any ceiling. I don't. And I don't think I ever did in my career.

I believe that every person, woman or man, is involved in fashion in some way. There are a few basics of our needs in life. We need to have a roof over our head, we need to have food, and we need to put something on our backs every day. And so, to some degree or another, we're all involved in fashion. Fashion doesn't have to be only on the runway, it's whatever we are wearing that day, and believe it or not, we all make a considered choice to wear a particular item or not.

You know what I love wearing? Fishnets. We only used to wear them in the clubs, not that I was in a club very often, but it was something we wore onstage only. Fishnets make your legs look really great, especially the tight fishnets. They're not too comfortable on the bottom of the feet, especially by the end of the day. But fishnets can just make you feel great, and quite honestly when you feel sexy there's also a little bit of kick and pep in your step, and just a power within you. And so fishnets give you that little pep in your step, and I like that. I find that some people like to wear short skirts, and if short skirts look good on you, all power, do it.

I find that for me my power style is stiletto heels. Sometimes they are a little bit painful, I have to admit—um, so is life. My first pair of Manolo Blahniks, I was working at *Vogue* at the time, and that day the doctor said, "Yes, you are in menopause." And I thought, *That's it*, M *for Menopause*, M *for Manolo, I'm going out and buying my first pair*, and I did. And I have been wearing them ever since. So I think, do what you want to do. Whatever makes your socks go up and down, just do it.

Colleen in her Florida home office

A few years ago, I did all the things you'd never expect. Met a guy—Match.com—decided to get married, a month later we moved to Tampa, had new jobs, a house, no furniture, three new stepchildren, a whole new environment. Talk about mix it up, it was wild.

I am working at sales for a major newspaper, the *St. Petersburg Times,* the largest daily newspaper in Florida. And I work in business development and love every day. It's just fantastic. And my husband is the vice president of USF Health and the dean of the College of Medicine for the University of South Florida. So I find myself in a role that I never expected. I was a professional career woman, I did my own thing, I had a great life, I was in New York. It was all about work and very single-focused. And now I have my career, but we laugh because I work full-time as a corporate wife as well, which is a whole new experience when you never aspire to do that. Anyone can take on the role, but if it's not been your goal, it's much more of a psychological change. Anything that you do as a corporate spouse, you have done in your career. I've done parties for one hundred people. I've entertained high-level dignitaries or celebrities or clients, but to do it all for someone else—while my husband certainly considers me a partner, and everyone we meet considers us to be a great team, it's a different role than you expected. And I feel at peace with it in a good way, and am able to accept that I'm in as powerful a role in that position as I am in my own career, which is based on not just my being comfortable with it, but having had a little success with it, too. Isn't that always the way?

I see a difference in terms of what people are wearing to work, now that I'm not in the fashion industry. I still never wear a suit, but people I work with do. I'm not ready to go there yet. My look has remained the same. I believe I dress very femininely. To my conservative bosses, I probably dress very casually. I don't think so. I recognize that I might be pushing the edge of the envelope a little bit, because the rest of the world, I think, is moving in that direction.

I also find myself, in the corporate spouse role, as someone that people do notice and make comments on what I'm wearing. I haven't figured out if it's because they want to be nice. If you're The Wife Of, everyone is trying to be nice. I understand that, I recognize it. They also know me as a woman who worked at *Vogue,* and I must *know,* whether I do or not.

What I wear to events in my corporate spouse role is usually driven by what I've worn to work during the day, unlike what I should be wearing for that event. And I found myself kind of caught short a couple of times. I'm just thinking of my workday versus *Oh, we're going on a boat tonight.* Everybody else here is in casual boat clothes and I'm in my skirt. I look a little goofy. Well, I'll just wear my flip-flops. I'll try to fit in. When you're in that position, just go with it. What can you do? They probably know I'm coming from work, and I want that. I have to have my own career. That's what gives me that center.

What makes me powerful? I wear thin. Being thin gives me such a power surge that I can do anything. I look back to the times when I have been the most successful in either career, personal, whatever it was, I was thin. It's hard to admit that thin is it. I've been not thin. I've been thinner. I've been heavy. I've been all the variations. The power surge is at thin. You get the vibe, you get the smile, and you are energized by it. Or I am, anyway. It's an addiction in that sense. Once you feel the high in anything, you want more of it. It's like having that right power suit. You can't wear the same suit every day. And the vibe off every suit is not always the same. So I'm always shooting for thin. I wear thin.

Once you have enough equity built up in yourself, you could be a little more honest in saying that. I know it's not what mothers want to hear for their sixteen-year-olds, that that's what's gonna give them the confidence. But what really gives you self-esteem is something that you have done, something you have accomplished, something you have worked for. And I've done that. Having already had that as a base, I can now say thin. If I didn't have that as a base, and felt that thin was my base, that's not enough for anybody. The accomplishment is really where you're starting from to be able to have good self-esteem. That's the beginning of then being able to recognize that thin makes me feel really powerful.

When you have power, you just know it. I'm in powerful positions, have been, am now. When you ask me the question *When do I feel powerful?* Every day. It's just part of me. It's from the time when my boss is teasing me, "Oh," you know, "who're you having dinner with tonight? The mayor or the people who are the billionaires in town?" And I just throw it back at him. "Actually, tonight they're coming over for cocktails. We're just gonna sit around." Which is a powerful position, and I'm not intimidated by it any longer, I'm not even fazed by it. It's just what it is. When you're thrust in those positions, you just go with it.

Elizabeth Garlington

Nashville, Tennessee | October 2002

Mine's a sad story. In November 1991, we had a house fire. Two of my little spaniels jumped up on the oven to get some Fig Newtons and turned the oven on, and the house was almost totally destroyed. At the time, I was married for four years. The dream I had before we married, two days before my wedding day, was I was on a very bright red, highly shellacked seesaw. I was on the top, but nobody was at the other end, and I was in a very tattered wedding dress, and I had on really dirty high-top Converse All Star tennis shoes, and my hair was pulled back like I had just played tennis or something. And if I had listened to that dream, I would never have married him.

So what happened four years into the marriage was I was lonely, not alone, but lonely. Had the house fire. My mother then became involved in my personal life. She was helping me reconstruct this house while my husband never offered anything. My mother came over one day and she said, "What the fuck is going on in your life?" And I started crying.

My younger brother was engaged to the daughter of a major person that you would know everywhere you turn. And they were having an

Trappings interview portrait,
Elizabeth D. M. Wise's home

engagement party at the Piedmont Driving Club in Atlanta. And I will preface this with I am from a very old, aristocratic, *Southern* family. I asked my husband would he accompany me to this huge engagement party. It was huge, huge. Jane Fonda was there. He told me that morning that he would not go. And I've learned since that just because your partner does not want to go, it's the duty of the relationship to go. Not to go to go, but to go to support your partner.

And for the first time in four years of that marriage I thought, *It's okay to be alone*. And I remember assembling my clothes. I was in the bathroom with my makeup. It was like an artist, and I am an artist in my professional life. I had my makeup like Way Bandy designing your face. I had the palette constructed, and I had it sequential, and I had it chronologized. And I put on black underwear. It was brand-new, too—the bra was sixty bucks. I bought the most expensive stockings I could find. I bought Chanel sling-back pumps. Probably some retribution involved in that charge. And I put on my makeup and I thought, *What's missing?*

I was very close to my grandmother. She passed away four years ago. My grandmother would see me in my baseball hat and my bib jean overalls and my high-tops and she would think something was horribly wrong with my life because I did not look like I could go to lunch with her at the club. My grandmother always said, "You never know who you are going to meet at the grocery store. Where is your lipstick, darling?" So I had bought some new lipstick, Lancôme, thirty dollars a pop. I mean, I went on a little spending binge that morning. And I'm putting on my makeup and my hair is done. *What is missing?* And I had on all black. There is something very sensible about black. I don't think it's a color of mourning, I think it's the color of *You better look at me and you better look at my face.*

I put on the pearls, and I told my friend that these really were armor for me. And they're my grandmother's. I put the pearls on, and I looked at myself, and I was really, really alone. It was the first time I realized after four years in a marriage, not so much a battering marriage, but a very lonely experience, that I was in it alone.

I walked out the door. I got in my car and I'm driving up Peachtree Road to the driving club and I pulled into the porte cochere. I told the gentleman who opened my car door, I said, "Wish me a lot of luck, babe, 'cause I need it tonight." He said, "You all by yourself tonight, babydoll? Where's your man?" I said, "He ain't here anymore, I'm by myself." He said, "You'll do fine."

I walked down the big corridor into the club, and there's a big, huge, gold, gilt mirror in the hallway, and I stopped and I looked at myself in my finery and it was costuming at its best. And I looked at myself and I said, I'll never forget, I said, "It's showtime!" I walked up the two steps, into the marble foyer with the gold chandelier and the marble walls and the Oriental rugs and all the trappings that you ever think of aristocracy, and I was alone. It didn't really matter how much money I did or didn't have, I was alone. It didn't matter.

I walked into the party, and the first person I see is Robert Redford. My mother and father were standing there and saw me come down the steps, alone. My mother later told me she said to my father, "She's alone again, that son of a bitch." Well, I made my debut that night. Then legally I was divorced sixty days later. So my armor has always been denim, blue jean jackets, a ten-dollar bill in my pocket, and a pair of sunglasses. And if I really have to put on something, it's always black and it's always pearls.

Anne Barry

Jersey City, New Jersey | August 2004

I have to say frankly, when I first heard about your project, it totally turned me off because clothes mean nothing to me. And power, I don't think of feeling powerful. Power is an aftereffect of doing. I just got back from Quilting by the Lake. I have in my time made some cozy bed coverings, but Quilting by the Lake attracts virtually all women, all middle-aged and up, who do art quilts, studio quilts.

Something funny happened at Quilting by the Lake. I had a dream. It was on the fourth night. I got balls. It was just amazing. It was so funny I almost laughed in the dream. It was Technicolor, it was gorgeous. I didn't have any clothes on, and I had this beautiful, deep rosy pink scrotum. And you know, in a dream you can do funny things. I got out of my body and went around behind myself to take a look. And there it was. Beautifully shaped, not wrinkly and ugly and purpley and hairy.

Trappings interview portrait,
Grace Church Van Vorst

Virtually hairless, really attractive. And sort of just gently swinging. And I thought, *These are terrific!* So then I was a little curious, of course, so I raced around front and looked, and no male appendage, no penis envy here. I was me, but I had balls. And I thought, *This is just wonderful.* Before lunch, this is all over the campus. Everybody loves this dream.

Power is kind of an afterthought word, but it's whatever is meaningful and strong. Strength is a better word than power. I guess power goes with the penis, not with the balls. Ah dear. There's a great dream, I'll tell you. Every time I doubt myself, I remember I've got balls.

Anne at work

Stephanie Pierce

Albion, Michigan | March 2005

I have to admit, I spent the last week thinking about this project and what I would say in my interview. I've gone back and forth with myself trying to decide if I was actually gonna go through with it. I'm not worried about the camera or about talking about myself, but I have felt a deep-seated discomfort with the project, and I spent a week thinking about why and what I wear that makes me feel powerful, and I couldn't come up with anything. And I finally realized that I'd been agonizing about it because there are no clothes that I have ever owned, currently own, or will ever own that will make me feel powerful. People buy certain clothes to reflect their identities, and others react to how people are dressed by making assumptions about them or treating them in a certain way. I know I do, and I'm certainly not the only one in America that does. I'm a part of this culture. I interact with it every day. I have no choice but to interact with it. Complete rejection of the culture is an interaction with it just like complete embracement would be.

Trappings interview portrait,
Lynne Chytilo's home

28

This is a trap of sorts that we all live in, men and women alike. Men are as trapped by their trappings as women are. And even though I feel that our society is still in balance in favor of the unambiguously gendered male, I feel sorry for men, as I do for women. None of us can escape the power our clothes have to speak before we actually do. And no matter what statement my clothing makes about me, even if it's a positive statement, it doesn't make me feel powerful, it makes me feel the opposite of powerful. Whenever I start to really think about clothing, I just kinda feel depressed.

Yeah, I love to put on a pair of holey jeans one day if I'm feeling like being vintage-y cool. Or the next day I'll wear the same one if I feel just like being comfortable and lazy. I have my own style. I have things I like to wear and things I wouldn't ever be caught dead in. But clothes don't make me feel anything I'm not already feeling. Except sometimes maybe uncomfortable. Clothes have the power to make me into someone else to the people around me even if I'm not somebody else, even if I'm still me. When people react to my clothing, they aren't reacting to my power. They're reacting to the power our culture gives to objects that people own as opposed to the people that own those objects. The only power I have in relation to clothes is a false power. When I really think about it, clothes make me feel powerless.

I feel like a true American materialist because I know that in this culture clothes do matter, clothes do speak for you even if you try to buck the system. And it doesn't feel like power to me to know that even though I want my clothes to stop talking, I can't make them. And even though I think of all this, I still don't hate clothes 'cause it's not their fault. I really like some clothes and wouldn't want to wear a burlap bag even if it did the same job. I'm a product of my culture even though I obviously don't like a lot of it. And that's that. It's inevitable.

I'm not gonna spend my nights crying about it and feeling bad and staring in the dark. I don't mean to be a total downer, it's just that I love clothes and I really, really hate them at the same time. They're fun to play with and wear, but they don't ever make me feel powerful.

Jenny Sanborn

Santa Fe, New Mexico | July 2005

I believe that clothes are powerful. I wore a couple of things tonight that make me feel powerful. Glitter makes me feel incredibly powerful. I teach violence prevention, I teach full-contact self-defense, but I also believe I should be able to wear glitter. They're not mutually exclusive. I think being powerful is about embracing humor. I think humor is incredibly powerful. And that's what glitter means to me, it means being a little light, being able to have fun while still working to solve some of the world's most pressing problems.

My shirt makes me feel powerful. It's the color of chocolate. Embracing what I love, what makes me feel good, makes me feel powerful. I also have on a ring that a dear friend gave me about fifteen years ago. We decided that every woman should have a big, chunky, sassy, don't-fuck-with-me ring. It also represents friendship with women, which makes me feel incredibly powerful. If it wasn't for the women in my life, I wouldn't be where I am today. Whenever I need that little extra umph in my day, I put on that ring.

I also have on a necklace from my grandmother. It's an abalone necklace that belonged to her mother. She is eighty-nine years old, still does water aerobics at the Y twice a week. Throughout my entire life, she has been my hero. She divorced my emotionally abusive, and I think physically abusive, grandfather at age fifty at a time where women weren't getting divorced. And she started her life from scratch, refused to live a life filled with oppression and violence and self-doubt. So when she gave me this gift, it made me feel incredibly powerful.

Jeans make me feel incredibly powerful. I feel like I can do anything in jeans. I've traveled throughout the world in jeans, I've worked in jeans, I have prevented a kidnapping in jeans.

Five years ago, I had a man attempt to kidnap me in Santa Fe. At eight o'clock on a Tuesday morning as I was walking down the street, he was in his car, in this very quiet residential neighborhood. As soon as I felt him look at me, I knew something was wrong. My gut, which we're taught not to trust, told me, *Something is wrong*. He continued down the block out of sight, turned around, blocked my access to the sidewalk, grabbed my arm, and tried to take me with him. I had taken a self-defense class eight years before in college, and it saved my life. Before my brain even knew what was happening, my body was responding. I broke his grip, threw my hands up, and said, "Do not touch me." And that was enough. I was not the victim that this guy was anticipating. So he's looking around for witnesses and he's fleeing, and I'm managing my adrenaline, getting five out of the six digits on his license, and reporting him to the cops. They caught him because two weeks later he carjacked a nineteen-year-old woman at knifepoint outside a local mall. He had a knife to her throat and he said, "If you scream I'm going to fucking kill you." He had gotten her into his car, was driving. She was in the passenger seat and she just jumped out. She trusted her gut and jumped out of the moving vehicle.

After that experience, I made a serious personal and professional commitment to teaching these skills to as many people as I can. I teach full-contact self-defense because of my political beliefs that women should live a life free from fear. That we should not be looking around every corner for something that might happen to us. That we should not limit ourselves because of our fears and our lack of believing that we can take care of ourselves and protect ourselves.

The attempted kidnapping was going to change my life dramatically. I could have become a person, a woman, filled with fear, filled with doubt. What was amazing was, one of the most frightening, upsetting, daunting experiences of my life became one of the most positive experiences I've ever, ever had. I was able to see for myself that I can defend myself. Women's two top fears: rape and murder. Okay? Men's biggest fear: public humiliation. Okay? I know so many women go through life with this fear, What would I do if someone tried to grab me, if somebody tried to rape me? It's unfortunate, but I had this opportunity to see how strong I was. And how powerful I was. And

Trappings interview portrait,
Santa Fe Art Institute

that nobody had the right to violate me. So it's become totally positive. I work with children ages six to twelve. I work with teen girls and boys. I work with adult women. I just taught a class for wheelchair users, from a wheelchair, because everyone has the right and the ability to defend themselves. And I have to say it is great, but I'm not empowering other people. I'm creating an opportunity for them to empower themselves. You have to do it for yourself.

I'm an anthropologist by training, so I'm always there, sort of, you know, pushing those cultural limitations and boundaries to see what people accept and what they don't accept. What's the boundary, you know? Why is it acceptable for a fourteen-year-old girl to show where she's been waxed and where hair should be naturally and it's not?

This is a fashion line that I have invented called Fur Her. I decided to invent this so it can be put in the pants and just have a little bit peeking out there. So instead of just trying to avoid making a statement, you can actually really make a statement. It's specifically for the younger set, who seem absolutely obsessed with low-rider pants. Which I find to be anathema. They're always so low, you know they have been waxing, they've been preening, they've been doing whatever. My idea is to come up with a line of different colors, different textures. Just show it. You know? Instead of just pretending like it's not there, just see it. Own it. This is my way of protesting, with a little humor, a little pink, because a lot of young girls say, This is how I find my power, showing a lot of skin. My generation has a little bit of trouble with that. And I'm sort of questioning, who has the power?

I think as girls and women, we're taught what makes us powerful is helping other people, giving of ourselves, reaching out, prioritizing others. Even in my generation, that's been this huge push. I've had to really evaluate that in the work that I do. How can I work for community empowerment but also take care of myself? How can I do this and make a living wage? How can I do this and get health insurance? How can I do this and get a filling at the dentist when I need to and not have to put it on my credit card? It's really brought up a lot of empowerment issues for me.

But obviously the bottom line is I feel like I'm creating a community where people respect themselves, and value themselves, and they're gonna respect and value other people. Looking into somebody's eyes and having them say, you know, "Thank you so much, I'm a totally different woman than when I walked into this room." I get goose bumps talking about it. It's incredibly powerful.

I'm in a big transition in my life. I have decided to sort of step away from the work that I've been doing. I have decided to head to Costa Rica for two months. A lot of people are sort of projecting their own stress about their lives and their jobs onto me. I saw a saying somewhere once that said, "Those who've abandoned their dreams will discourage yours." That's been a message that I've been thinking about a lot. 'Cause I don't ever want to abandon mine or discourage anybody else's. So I'm pushing that to the side and going for it. If I'm not working in the nonprofit world, who am I? If I'm not working with women's community groups, who am I? And this is a chance for me to figure that out.

Jenny pumpin' gas in her Fur Her

The last time I saw you, I was preparing to go to Costa Rica. I sold most of my things, my vehicle, I wanted to be prepared for anything. I headed down there in January of 2006, came back at the end of June. I was doing English language teaching in a really small town called El INVU las Peñas Blancas. You probably won't find that on the map. I lived in a town of five hundred people, I think there were about a thousand cows, so that kind of gives you an idea of what the population was. I was teaching English to people in the town who maybe had never made it past the first or second grade, and then teaching people who are involved in the tourist industry in a four-star resort. Working with people who were in maintenance, housekeeping, working in the kitchen, and then I also had the chance to work with upper management. But they all had a common goal of improving their English to provide a better life for themselves and their family. That was their common goal that everybody had.

I'm so glad I went! It really forced me to look at what I wanted out of life. So from this I learned that I don't have to travel to find these kinds of challenges for myself in my life. If I live in the same place for ten years, I can still create that sense of being present, and not knowing what's behind every corner in my daily life, and not get caught in a rut.

I had spent the last ten years of my life working for social justice, working with nonprofit organizations, and very willingly sacrificing things, giving of myself, accepting things that were maybe less than I deserved because I was doing what I loved and I was helping people. So I really had to take a step back and say, *Who am I if I'm not doing this?* You know, what's the payoff? It's certainly not the money. And that's why I'm excited about what I'm doing now, 'cause I'm teaching, which is helping, but I'm also starting my own business, which means doing things on my terms, creating opportunities for myself.

My new business is teaching English as a second language to employees in the hospitality industry. It's about teaching job skills and life skills at the same time. It's not only language training, it's about cultural fluency. You know, how can somebody from another country understand not just the spoken language, but what's the body language saying? What's the distance between us saying? Is eye contact appropriate right now or is it not appropriate? For me the whole goal is to reduce the stress that non-English-speakers feel in an English-speaking world.

And I still feel like it's true to my commitment to social justice and helping people. I also teach Spanish to English speakers. For me it all fits within this bigger picture of creating an environment of communication, which I feel also facilitates a community of peace and openness and understanding, which right now in this political climate I think is the most necessary thing.

I do get a lot out of it. It feels amazing to me to look out at my students with these huge smiles on their faces after they've been able to create a sentence in a language other than their own. But also, I'm realizing it's what I'm getting in return. You know, so, *Who am I when I'm not helping?* is *Who am I when I'm able to receive?* and being open to getting something in return. But I think the trip to Costa Rica was what it took. So there is also that hope for me of *Who am I when I'm not helping?* and *Who am I when I have abundance?* 'Cause I always thought poverty was very noble. I got really used to that, you know? But all the people I work with want a higher quality of life, and they say, "Jenny, it's okay to want that."

Jenny teaching English at Santa Fe Community College

Kathleen Ferguson

Jersey City, New Jersey | August 2004

My mother expected me to take the veil, if you understand my drift, but not quite like this. My mother thought I was going to be a nun. I teach Middle Eastern culture and dance to the women here at the senior center. In Western culture, women seem to be throwaways after a certain age—we're not worth as much as, say, pretty young thing. So I always teach that a pretty girl is an accident of nature. A beautiful woman is her own creation. I teach that we are women, not little girls. We are wise because the years and experience that God's given us have made us so much more than pretty. We are beautiful. And we are wonderful.

When women first come into my class, sometimes they're very shy and they don't know quite what to expect. My job is to bring out that inner woman, that inner talent, and that beauty that is inside. Because all real beauty comes from within, and we're just learning how to express it physically. Dance is a discipline, we're not just flopping all over the place. Each woman has a different style of movement.

This is my power outfit. This is my teaching leotard because it's easier for the women to see what I'm doing with the arms, with the shoulders. When I dance with the ladies, we're properly covered up within all Middle Eastern standards; no one can complain that we're overexposed. All of the geegaws and doodads bring us into

You won't find a "shrinking violet" here.

Trappings interview portrait, Grace Church Van Vorst

another culture, help bring us psychologically to a different place. We are on Cleopatra's barge going up the Nile. We are more than housewives, more than grandmas. We don't sit in front of the TV watching Jerry Springer and knitting socks. We work very hard in our class.

My idea is to bring out what most people think seniors can't do. There are women who work harder than I do in this class. The openness that so many of them have to the culture itself—we pass books around about women in this culture, how they do have everything but freedom, and how lucky we are that we can put this on, but we can take it off and go about our business. I find that we have built a sisterhood very much like the Middle Eastern families do. Women dance with their sisters-in-law. That's who you live with, you bond with the women. These are your friends. As seniors, most of us are alone, and this is where we come to bond. We bicker, we bicker, we argue, but it's just like any other family, and I find that I've found a new family here that allows me to give what I have inside and share it with other people who do appreciate it. When I see these women who have come in like shrinking violets, and they're up there dancing now, that really gives me a sense of empowerment because I know that I've given something of myself to them and brought out what is best in them. And that is my pleasure, and my joy, and my empowerment.

Linda Davis

Sheridan, Wyoming | April 2004

You know they say clothes make the woman, but sometimes I think it takes the woman to make the woman.

I have never really felt powerful. I've felt good about what I'm doing, but never extremely powerful about what I wear. I think the closest to feeling powerful is when I hit that big round number and decided to quit my job of thirty-seven and a half years and start an art gallery. That's the closest to either being stupid or powerful, I'm not sure which, that I have ever become. I like dressing. I like looking nice, but I also feel really good in my jeans and my sweatshirt that has DAVIS GALLERY across the front of it.

It was a family business that I was working in where the son got all the stuff and the daughters didn't get any, but yet I worked there. I stayed there for thirty-five and a half years. Mother always said, "If you want to leave this shop, do it and it'll be wonderful." And I had the full support of my two sisters. It was hard to tell my brother. He wasn't real thrilled, but that's the way it goes. He is very proud of what I'm doing. It took a lot of courage to quit a job that was steady and had a good paycheck coming in. And then try to go to a bank and have them say, How old are you, you want how much money, and you're a woman? It's hard. It's real hard to do that.

I've always loved art. I wanted to go to

Trappings interview portrait,
Lynn Reeves's Home

39

college when I graduated from high school, but my dad at that time thought the girls should either get married or work at the business for the rest of their life. College was not an option that was presented to me. You don't talk about it.

I didn't know how to cut a mat when I started the gallery. I learned how to cut a mat, and now I can just, you know, whip it right out. And then all of a sudden the artists started coming in with things. It's just been awesome. You know what it is, it's just a dream come true. I just hated to have to wait so long to have it come to fruition. But I will work as long as I can. I may be eighty years old and still cutting mats. There's not a lot of people that can say that they love every minute of their work. I mean, you can put up with it and you can do it and you can kind of like it and like it a little bit, but love it every day? I feel really fortunate now.

A dream come true at Davis Gallery

40

Tina Camero

Jersey City, New Jersey | August 2004

Now that I am six months pregnant, what makes me feel powerful is wearing my own clothes and not having to wear maternity clothes. I have a little story, I guess, that I wanted to share about being pregnant and wearing clothes that make me feel powerful. It's all gonna kinda come back to wearing all black, because if I wasn't pregnant, I would answer, "Wearing all black makes me feel powerful."

I'm not married, and I'm doing this on my own. My family has been having a hard time with this. When I started to show, my family asked me to keep my pregnancy a secret. I internalized that and hid it from some people. Not a lot. All my friends knew. But they asked me to keep it from some family members, and with keeping a secret, I felt like I had to hide my pregnancy.

Going to work I wore clothes that were really big for me. When I couldn't button my pants or when I couldn't wear button-down shirts, I had to wear bigger clothes, clearly not showing my belly. I internalized that. I was feeling shameful for being pregnant, and going against my parents' values and their traditions. I was really starting to show, and being around my friends, my urban family, gave me support and just made me always feel blessed.

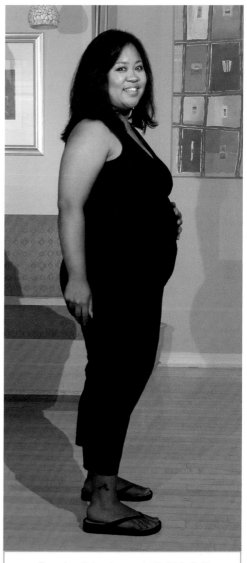

Trappings interview portrait, Ria's Café

I remember going to school wearing this t-shirt. I felt so good wearing a tight little t-shirt 'cause that's my style. I'm a high school counselor. I remember purposefully wearing all black and wearing my little t-shirt so that my belly could show. I felt really good about letting the students know, and teachers and administrators know, and letting my secret out.

I really thought that if I wore the t-shirt they would just ask, but nobody did. There was no reaction right away. I started to tell students, and the first few that I told were seniors, and what they did was they tried to protect me and they didn't tell anybody. I work in a small school, there're only two hundred students, and I thought it would go around school like that. And it didn't. Up until last year, our policy was to kick out any girls in the school who were pregnant. And I remember girls going to school and wearing the big shirts. Clearly we knew. I wanted to make sure they were okay, but I didn't want to say anything just because I knew that was

Tina with her daughter, Maida, and her mother, Sonia.

a policy. It has changed. The girls have every right to stay where they go to school, and there are alternatives for them if they choose.

My family's still having a hard time. My mom will soon see when she comes at the end of this month that I'm gonna be wearing tight clothes, and I'm gonna be wearing my own clothes, and even though she bought me lovely clothes from Motherhood, which I will wear in front of her, I will try to wear my own clothes for as long as I can. It's not gonna be much longer.

My mom, the day I told her, I remember her screaming on the phone, "We're having a baby! We're having a baby!" So she was excited, but there were still issues about me not being married. Between my parents there were things that they just didn't want to share with everybody. I actually still worry because not all my family knows. I'm feeling something that makes me not want to tell older people of my parents' generation. So I'm still very wary of that. I have family here in the area, and one of my aunts called me to tell me that my cousins are due in November and December. But I didn't tell her anything. It's that generation that I feel are maybe not judgmental, but not understanding.

Laura C. Hewitt

Ester, Alaska | June 2005

I'm an artist. I love life. I'm interested in all different aspects of it. I think that really experiencing actual life and death really enhances artwork. Experiencing life and death, it's just a lot different than supermarket shopping.

I bear bait and I bow hunt. You have to camouflage yourself completely. You can't use shampoo, perfume, deodorant. You shouldn't even be bathing or eating garlic or that type of thing. And you're sitting in a bait stand in camouflage clothing with mosquito net all over you. You're on a tree, so you're completely camouflaged.

I bow hunt up north of the Yukon River. It's bow hunting only, no guns, no four-wheelers, nothing like that. You pack in the bait. Like fifty, sixty pounds because you're feeding basically every bear in the woods because you're waiting for the larger bears to come in. At least I do, and I'm pretty picky about what size I'm gonna take out. The last one I got missed being a record by a half an inch. A lot of it is just sitting there being camouflaged and watching these bears, watching the little ones and the sows, which you don't want to take out, completely part of the tree.

I don't see or speak to another human being by e-mail or cell phone or anything for days and days at a time. Rarely do people spend that much time not communicating. So you really figure out how much of life performance is. When other people watch, you automatically go into a performance. And this is only a performance for myself.

I hunted with guns for many years. Guns you can do at a distance. It's pretty impersonal. Bow hunting is very up close and personal. You are right there with the animal, you're smelling it, you're seeing it. And, like I said, you camouflage yourself to the point where you are actually part of your environment. You're not even really a human being anymore. It's really primitive. So I got into bow hunting and I've never gone back. I actually do birds now by bow, too, which is really difficult and very expensive. Arrows are about sixty dollars each, and, you know, you miss and that arrow has arced off into just nowhereland. I have a dog trained that would retrieve birds, and now I'm training her to retrieve my arrows.

Two years ago I was hunting up north and I was treed by a grizzly bear. It's illegal to shoot a grizzly bear over bait. You can do black bear, but not grizzly bear. Up where it's bow hunting only, there's an element of a different kind of hunter that will sometimes take out a grizzly bear. If you get caught, they remove your license for many years. They might remove it forever, and they publicize the event because they want to trash the people that are doing that

Laura's installation *Winter Dreams*

Laura hand-building a ceramic pot
in her studio

Trappings interview portrait,
the Annex Gallery

type of thing. So I couldn't shoot the grizzly bear, even though it was charging me, because of that aspect. You could see the publicity: "Deaf Female Art Professor Makes This Terrible Error." Right? Forget it. I would rather die.

I have to quit smoking when I bear bait. That's the worst. I chew. So I was able to smell this bear. And I thought I saw a black bear coming in. Black bears on average up there are maybe five hundred to seven hundred pounds, and grizzlies go up to twelve hundred pounds. So I saw this black thing coming through the woods into the bait, and I thought it was the head of a black bear

Laura bow hunting north of the Yukon River

and it turned out to be the paw of a grizzly bear. It had a whole different attitude than black bears. Black bears are really elusive, like cats, and they'll do reconnaissance all around the bait stand before they'll actually come in to eat. This grizzly bear didn't care. They're kings of the jungle.

It was huge. It was enormous. And it saw me right away. There was no fooling it. It came to the base of my stand. I was about fifteen feet up. And you see them in the films, they have that trained grizzly bear that goes, "grr, grr," right? This one was like "RAAAHHHH!" at the base of the stand. It opened up its mouth, it peeled back its lips. It was like looking in the side of a freight car. It did this for two and a half hours and I had to watch. My bow felt like a flyswatter.

I was pretty insane with fear. Even after it was gone and it was okay to come down. I waited as long as I could. There's a point where you get out of the stand, you're totally helpless because your bow's on the ground and you're lowering yourself out. I got my bow and I knocked an arrow. You're really not supposed to run around the woods with a knocked arrow because you can trip or fall and put one through yourself, or your foot, or something really stupid. But I didn't care. I knocked out. I didn't run. I walked.

It makes me feel powerful to be able to camouflage that much and to know, really, how fragmented and how loose identity really is. We all sort of make ourselves up and become what we need to be. And I think that making my own clothes has become a part of that. In my artwork, I actually do a lot about camouflage and mimicry. I guess I worry about the normalization and homogenization of people. That we all wear the same clothes, we all eat the same food. We have a lot of the same experiences. My artwork really tries to transgress that by using direct experience to break open that type of value system.

Stephanie Rivera

Santa Fe, New Mexico | July 2005

I'm a patrol officer. I wear a lot of equipment. We have our regular weight plus forty-six pounds. We wear our bulletproof vests, magazines, Mace, baton, knife, gloves, handcuffs. What else do I have? My gun, and then this is my microphone to record when I go on traffic stops. This is a Taser. It incapacitates you without affecting your major organs or your brain. Your muscles basically just go into immediate spasm and you fall and cry and scream.

This is not powerful to me at all. All of this is a sign of authority. When I'm not here, this is not me. I want to look like a girl. I want my hair down. I want to be pretty. I want to smell nice. I don't wear perfume at work. I don't wear jewelry here except my wedding ring, and that's because my husband says so, or I wouldn't, because if I broke a finger, shit, I ain't gonna get it off. So my life here is not who Stephanie is. This is what I do for a living, this is how I make money, this is how I raise my family, and this is what I choose to do, but when I go home, this is not me. If you saw two pictures, you would never know that it was the same person.

I'm a mom. I'm a wife. I'm a woman. My kids don't see this. When I'm in it, they're like, Whatever, you're just my mom. I have to nurture them and do all those things that a mama's supposed to do. I have responsibilities to my husband. To be his best friend, to be his

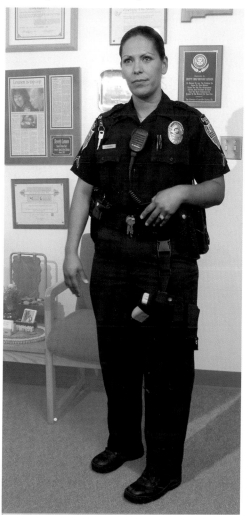

Trappings interview portrait, Chief Bev Lennon's office, Santa Fe Police Headquarters

lover, be his confidant. I have chores at home. I have responsibilities to my family.

Women cops are out of control. We are viciously smart, witty, beautiful, intelligent. We're everything that all the women behind us wanna be. We're not gonna be quiet. I think the majority of us become cops because we are so dominant in our skin. Our mamas raised us this way. Our heritage is this way. Spanish women are very strong and we're very dominant. Usually the woman of the household is the glue. Without the woman, the man would be nothing. Yeah, he makes the money and does the hard stuff and all the muscley stuff, but your mama's the glue. She's your strength to make you feel like first of all you're something, and you could be anything.

The women in my family are my role models, but I also go after the women in my culture. I am also inspired and empowered by them. Sometimes when I go to calls and I come to an elderly Hispanic woman, I immediately want to take to her and make sure, like, no one's gonna bother her. Those are the people that you immediately want to care for, the elderly and the children.

Stephanie (looking like a girl) with her daughter Jade

When you enter a typical Hispanic household, if I enter as primary, they usually respect us when we walk in. We have made a name for ourselves, that we will enforce the laws of this community and this country. But we have had a growing population of Mexican nationals. If I enter the room of a Mexican national and I'm in charge, I get no response from the man whatsoever. He won't even acknowledge that I'm in the room. He'll look to my guy partner and respond to him. My partner can be white, cross-eyed, and gay, and he will respond to him before he will even look at me twice. I will still demand respect and I will still take charge. And you still will get arrested by a girl.

You just have all kinds. When you show up, some men are so intimidated by you, they're tongue-tied. Like little second graders. They want to pull your hair 'cause they like you. They can't even respond to you because they're just like dumbfounded that you look the way you look. So you get all kinds. Every day. All day. And I think that's what makes us demented. You have to deal with all those layers, then I could be standing here doing this interview and the room could blow up and I have to go from stop to go. Adrenaline drops and rushes and it takes a toll on your body, it takes a toll on your soul, and it takes a toll on your heart and your mind and your sleep. You see and do what every other civilian doesn't want to see and do. We, ten hours a day, live horror. Children, sexual abuse. Dead people. Arms pulled off. Guts all over. Only the strong make it. You hope to God you make it sane.

My husband gets mad. "You don't even tell me what's going on." I'm like, "Dude, I've lived it for ten hours." You have to explain what part they need to be in. I've learned where to place things. When I'm hurting, I'll address you. I'll explain things to you. I'll tell you what I saw and why it makes my heart hurt. Why I can't sleep. You listen, but don't respond. Because my husband's not a cop, he's a construction worker. He has no idea. I don't want no Monday morning quarterbacking. I want you to listen, hug me. 'Cause I'm a woman. I'm your wife. I ain't a police officer. I just want it all to be gone. So that's his job. Make it all be gone. Having the ability to communicate and the ability to identify what's happening to you is the most powerful thing to survive. You have to. And if you can't do it, you won't last.

Carey Lovelace

Brooklyn, New York | October 2006

I'm a writer. I'm a playwright and an art critic, or an art critic and a playwright, depends on the crowd I'm running with. I am, right now, the way that I feel the most powerful, and I began to deconstruct why that is and what the elements are. And I realized the basic elements are black, leather jacket, interesting shoes that I can move around in easily, sculptural glasses.

I was trying to think about, like, what was it about black that I like besides the fact that I can drop soy sauce on my pants and, you know, I don't have to change them. I was trying to think why people in the art world wear black, and I was realizing that black is like a force. It's like a force of nature, it's a force of power. And when you sort of align yourself with black, it's like you're mysterious, you're coming from nowhere, it's a larger thing that you're kind of connecting to. There's actually something about the color black that's very forceful, you know? Then I was thinking, *Does it mean I want to be a mime?* No.

It's kind of like a uniform in a funny way. And I've always had this philosophy of clothing about men versus women. I've kind of looked down at men because I felt like, you know, men dress in uniforms. They like to dress alike: team clothes, gangs dress alike, businessmen dress alike. Men are always dressing alike. And women always like to differentiate themselves in terms of their dress, like the whole cliché is "Oh, we wore the same dress! Oh no, Oh no!" You know? So women are supposed to be unique whereas men are supposed to be the same, so I always kind of looked down at men as being, like, it's a lack of imagination. And then I was realizing that it's actually more powerful because when you are part of a group, you take the power of the group. You're more than yourself. I like wearing black because I'm part of a larger black-wearing community. A community of black-wearers which is larger than myself, sort of the aesthetic world going back for decades.

I love this coat. I just felt powerful even wearing the coat, you know? It's like hip, it looks like, you know, Patti Smith. But then I was thinking, and forgive me PETA, but it's the pelt of the animal. I'm wearing the animal pelt on my back. I'm taking the power of this animal and kind of wrapping myself in it without knowing it. I just feel kind of really great in this coat. And people can say really mean things to me, and it's just gonna kind of bounce off of me. And these particular pants, they're this sort of spongy material. They are also very pelt-like. I'm sort of dressed in this larger power.

I like these shoes. They're kind of edgy, they're comfortable. They kind of draw your eye downward. But then I was thinking, they're like bowling shoes, you're like part of the bowling team. You're part of the sports team, so it's the sports kind of power metaphor.

Then the final element was just these glasses. If I'm gonna wear glasses, I want to wear glasses that make a statement. I want glasses that just say, "I Am Glasses." You know? It's not a sort of a pretending, disappearing thing. I don't look myself in the mirror and see, you know, Marian the Librarian. I see a woman that has like red glasses on.

So it sort of sets the whole thing up. You have the red glasses, the green

Carey in her team colors

shoes, the pelt of the animal, the uniform, the darkness, and I am very powerful. I was asking myself, why do I feel better in this than I do in say, a Jil Sander suit or like an expensive, you know, Donna Karan this or that? And I was realizing, when I dress like that, I feel like an aesthetic object. And as an aesthetic object, I feel vulnerable. I feel like I'm being looked at, I'm a spectacle. When you are an object, people want to possess you. They want to have you, they want to destroy you. I feel a little bit self-conscious when I'm dressed up. I mean, it's nice, I look pretty, but I feel not powerful, you know? I feel pretty, I feel looked at.

And when I'm conscious of myself, I'm not being powerful. To me, power means having an effect on the world around me, being able to affect people, being able to affect events, and if I'm thinking about myself and how do I look, I feel like I'm not able to have that effect because my energy's kind of looping back inward. And I feel like that's a kind of a trap in a way. As a woman, I felt tricked into that a little bit. I could feel a certain kind of power, like over men, if I dressed a certain way, but it was a power that looped into itself, and it was a power in which at the end I was vulnerable because I wasn't really the active person in that transaction. Whereas when I'm here, like, channeling darkness, you know, I'm freer to move around and do things or be present or not be present.

Trappings interview portrait,
Martha Wilson's home

Marilyn M. Cuneo

Minneapolis, Minnesota | April 2004

I must say that your question has made me think an awful lot in the last few days, because I thought, *Well, I don't really dress to feel powerful.* At this stage of life, I don't really care that much about clothes. I just want to be comfortable, and then if I'm comfortable, I feel more powerful probably. I'm not really looking to be powerful. Then I had to think more about this question of power and how it relates to me. I was an only child, and as an only child I kind of lived within myself from the time I was young. I think I still do that, so I think that my life has been a journey of empowering myself as a person.

There's an inner power that comes with many of life's experiences. Your reaction to them, and the success or failure of what has happened to you, or anything that I learn, or anything that I see, all goes into some kind of an inner process that I digest. And I feel that that's my home. I live there, and wherever I go I'm at home, so I don't feel strange in other places. But then, there's the other aspect, I suppose, of any kind of power that influences outside of yourself. I went back to school and got degrees and taught at the university. And it was really teaching there that I began to see that I had some influence on others, and that is a powerful experience, of course.

But I still really, even then, was doing

Trappings interview portrait,
Dorothy Crabb's home

53

that more from inside out until I went to China at the Beijing Conference, the fourth United Nations World Conference on Women. And that experience of being in a town with thirty thousand other women was a life-changing event because all of a sudden I could feel the power that women have in the world, and could see it. And from being pretty cynical and depressed about the conditions in the world, which is easy to do, I really got some hope to see what was happening there. At that conference they had a Women in Black demonstration where a thousand women dressed in black marched against violence to women. That was a very moving experience, and started me off in a new direction.

We've tried to bring Women in Black to this area, so I'm dressed today as a Woman in Black. What they do is to stand in a silent vigil in public places in their cities to protest against the violence in general, or specific violence in their countries, or whatever form of violence that they wish to be protesting. Anyone can organize a Women in Black movement in their own communities. We encourage people to do that. It has spread throughout the world. And I think that standing in the middle of downtown Minneapolis with a sign, or in silence, or speaking to people to tell them about what we're doing, why we're there, is really a moving experience and one that allows you to feel powerful because you know you are there as a Woman in Black. And there are Women in Black standing everywhere in the world against violence in their communities.

So that is a different form of power, where you are in community with other people and you know that you're part of something much bigger than yourself that really has the potential to change the world. We have made signs like this for about sixteen different countries now; they tell about what the violence is in many different countries. We display them on the walls or march with them in parades to influence different kinds of people to do the same kinds of things. We have tried to encourage people to live without fear, believing that fear is the most negative thing in the world and we are constantly bombarded with it every day by the news and the papers and the politicians trying to make us afraid of everything.

So that's kind of my thinking about what do I wear to feel powerful. I realize now that I have moved from totally an inner kind of power search into a much wider, global, worldwide, cosmic-being way to feel connected to everyone else. And that's where the power lies.

Since there have been a lot of Mother's Day activities throughout the country, today we're kind of going to honor the mothers in the world and the countries that are at war.

We speak and we do rituals and other kinds of things besides silent vigils. There have been quite a few groups in the Twin Cities area. The United Methodist Women had a Thursday in Black, and some of the teachers in the schools have done it, and a lot of the peace and justice groups in churches pick it up, and the Unitarian Church also. So there have been quite a few, but not as successful as we'd like it to be. It really would be very effective, I think, if we could have small groups that, anytime there is some violence, appear there. That is happening a little bit on the north side of Minneapolis, where there are groups that are coming out every time there's violence. And we should be one of them.

You know, one has to do something. I'm hoping that they're like seeds germinating in the soil, and long after I'm gone, it'll all burst forth in a lovely, peaceful world. Too bad I'm going to miss it, 'cause it doesn't look as if it's going that way. You might as well just live your life the way you'd like the world to be and do what you can. And then go to the movies and play tennis and get rid of the depression. And don't listen to the news. I've had to give that up.

A lot of people feel helpless, depressed and helpless, and they don't know what to do. They're not radical people. This is something they will do. It's almost like wearing a mask, you know? You can just stand there quietly, you don't have to say anything, but it makes you feel as if you're a part of something, and that does

Marilyn, Dorothy Crabb, and other allies protesting in silence, downtown Minneapolis

make you feel better. And powerful. There are a lot more shy people than aggressive, outgoing people. And a lot of them, you know, haven't even expressed themselves about the way they feel. But they do come forth quietly and put their names down and want to be called to do this.

The Women in Black began in Israel when women from Israel and Palestine met in 1988 to come together to try to protest against the occupation of the Palestinian lands. That's still going on there. We don't hear much about it, but it is still going on there.

Then, in the early nineties, the movement was taken up in Belgrade, where the women were protesting the horrors of what was going on there in the former Yugoslavia. And they went out into the public plaza every week for years. And that has become the center for the Women in Black movement, and they have an annual convention of people, although this is not an organization, it is just a movement.

Of course, there are all the other Women in Black around the world, and many of them began before they were Women in Black—the mothers at the Plaza de Mayo in Argentina. They began about 1977. And they're still at it! A lot of these groups are old. Then the Beijing Conference, where there were so many women in 1995, and a very huge Women in Black vigil there. All those women who were at that went home and started making their own Women in Black groups. We try to do that when we go around to speak. We try to encourage everyone that we talk to to start their own groups because that's what really would be most effective, if there are a lot of different, small groups around on all the street corners and neighborhoods.

Marcia B. Blacksmith

Lodge Grass, Montana | May 2004

I'm a senior here at Lodge Grass High School. My parents are Larry and Jackie Blacksmith. I have two sisters and two brothers. I'm the youngest of five. School is tough this year 'cause senior year is very demanding. You have to get your priorities straight. If you don't, then you'll just slack and not even realize that it's important that you get your grades up.

After I graduate I was gonna take a year off 'cause school is just very, very stressing. I wanna go to the Air Force. I have to talk to my uncles first, because my oldest sister tried to go to the Air Force, but they wouldn't let her. I wanna try to convince them that I wanna go. That I need to go. I was talking to the recruiter and he said that out of all the seniors, the reason why I wanted to go to the Air Force was the best. I said they would help me mentally, physically, verbally, and emotionally to deal with people in psychology. Because that's what I wanna go into. I even wanna get my doctorate in psychology. A lot of people were like, "It's hard. You won't do it. You won't make it." But, you know, I wanna prove 'em wrong. And another thing that I wanna do is go into creative writing, but right now my plans just keep changing every day almost.

I like wearing shirts that say stuff. A lot of people just laugh. 'Cause I have another one that says MY BOYFRIEND IS CUTER THAN YOURS. And I have one that says I MAKE BOYS

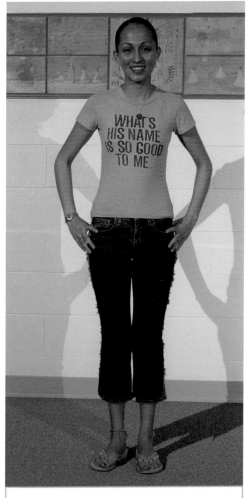

Trappings interview portrait,
Lodge Grass High School

CRY. I just have certain things on my shirt all the time. Most of the time it just expresses my individuality. It just expresses who I am.

Well, around here it's just everyone is everyone. But sometimes people criticize if you're different. What I believe is that you're yourself, and no one can change that. People always say, "Never change for the world, let the world change for you." But how can you not change when nothing stays the same? You know? It's not hard to be an individual. It's just hard to wanna fit in. I mean, why wanna fit in when you can just be yourself? And later on down the road when you're successful they'll realize, like, "Man, you know, I wish I could've hung out with her in high school, but I just ignored her." That's just kinda how things are in high school, though.

Marcia dancing to a Crow-style double beat at the MSU–Billings Powwow during her reign as Miss Crow Nation

Well, my sense of power is just being Indian. Being Crow and also Lakota. That just makes me stronger because in history Lakota and Crows were enemies back in the day. People just make a big deal out of it. And I'm also Irish. We're doing our family trees, and I found out that I'm Hidatsa and French. I was 2003 Miss Crow Nation. A lot of people were teasing me. They were like, "Our Miss Crow Nation's not even Crow! She's Sioux." But that's just who I am. I guess my personal power is just kinda having a personality. You know? Being able to laugh about things that get people down.

I've been wanting to be Miss Crow Nation since I was a little girl. I was like, "Yeah. I'm gonna be the 2002 and 2003 Miss Crow Nation." And they were like, "Yeah, whatever, whatever." I was like, "For real. Watch, I'll be Miss Crow Nation that year." When I got the title they were like, "You weren't even kidding, you did it!"

It's just a title that some girls hold throughout the year from the time they are picked to the end of Crow Fair. It's a pageant. It's kind of hard because you have to know your culture, your Crow language, the backgrounds of you, and then the importance of knowing the clan system. I think it was really challenging being Miss Crow Nation 'cause you powwow a lot. I traveled to twenty-two powwows since I got the title of Miss Crow Nation last year.

I have a lot of role models. One is my dad. He really worked hard to go back to college, and two years ago he graduated from college. He teased about it, too. He was like, "Yeah, I went on my twenty-year plan. I finally succeeded!"

Another one is SuAnne Big Crow. She's always been my role model ever since I found out who she was. She was such a strong young lady, and she was the best basketball player on the Pine Ridge Reservation. She got picked for the all-state South Dakota All-Stars team. I think she was the only Native American on that team. And a couple weeks before that tournament she was going home from practice and she got killed by a drunk driver. The sad thing about it was that she was against drugs and alcohol. Another one is Lori Piestewa. She was the first Native American woman, actually the first woman, to be killed in combat [in Iraq]. And my grandma. All them have always been my role models.

Donna Henes,

affectionately known as Momma Donna

Brooklyn, New York | October 2005

I'm a shaman. I'm wearing some ritual clothes because certainly these do make me feel powerful. For me power is authority, and authority as in authorship, and I am the author of my own life. But also as a shaman, I do macro-micro cosmic travel. I feel that I'm in connection with the cosmic forces. These are not street clothes, these are ritual clothes, and I never cross the two. These clothes have always helped me do my work because people don't see me, they see a shaman or they see spirit or they see something, but it's not about me. It's about something bigger than me.

I had a major vision about thirty years ago that kind of cemented me on this path. It was of Spider Woman. I had a momentary gestalt-knowing of how the universe is inextricably interconnected, and therefore what I was supposed to do was to weave and reweave this connection. So that everything I do, all the ritual work that I do, all the writing work that I do, has to do with establishing ways people connect with each other in community to connect with the greater universe that's bigger than us. And to connect with their own deeper, best, inner-self, and I feel that that's my mandated job. This is my job. Like it or not, pay the rent or not, I have no choice. This is what I have to do.

Years and years and years ago, I did a ritual for the halfway point of fall. It was a three-day, three-night vigil that started on Halloween night and went to All Saints Day and through All Souls Day, or Día de los Muertos. I was outside the whole time, and I didn't sleep the whole time, and I fasted the whole time, and people kept saying to me, "Aren't you scared to be out in the street by yourself in the middle of the night?" I kept thinking, *Who's going to bother me?* You know, who would possibly ever bother me? Nobody would ever bother me, and that's been the case. Nobody ever bothers me.

I also have power jewelry, specifically this ring, which is a brass ring. I've worn this for probably thirty years since I did a ceremony to marry myself, and this is probably my most powerful piece of accoutrement because it always reminds me of who I am, and what I'm doing, and my role and my path, and my so-called job in the world. My necklace is from Tibet. It's amber and brass and clearly powerful. Where I really shop is at the Salvation Army or any thrift shop. So consequently, I don't know the history of things and I kind of shop with my hands, you know? And I feel the energy, and so sometimes something is beautiful and I just, ooh, I can't touch it.

The other thing that's sort of a power ritual is the nail polish. I've always worn nail polish, and back in the day when feminists did not wear nail polish, I had a lot of grief about wearing nail polish. But for me, it never had anything to do with beauty or cosmetic, it has to do with power. They represent the fur-thest reach of my aura. They're always copper because copper is the perfect element of con-ductivity, and I feel like that helps me to stay conducted. So all of this is my ritual parapher-nalia, as it were, and when I wear this hat I know that I am in a ritual state and in that state the power just comes through me.

Trappings interview portrait, Martha Wilson's home

I've just written a book called *The Queen of Myself,* and it's for midlife women. I've talked to a lot of women in writing this book, and I came to realize that the women who feel invisible as they age are women who somehow want to feel invisible. And it's had the opposite effect on me. Not too long ago, some guy yelled out of a truck at me saying, "Looking good." And you know, my first reaction was *Oh my God, I never thought I would hear that again.* And then I instantly felt feminist guilt, like *Oh, you shouldn't think like that,* you know, *That creep.* But then I realized it was very different because he was not disrespecting me. It came out of an ultimate respect. It was like, oh, you looked in the mirror before you left the house kind of thing, you know? And I do dress, I've always dressed, always costuming.

Clothes never were about fashion for me or about style for me, but about power. I had this meeting with who I thought was gonna be my publisher at the time, and I came out of the

Eggs on End: Standing on Ceremony
Donna is blessing the altar before an Equinox Ceremony,
which she performed at the World Trade Center for seventeen years

meeting feeling really good, and I feel like I looked really good, too. I must have been smiling, and I walked to the Herald Square subway station at rush hour in the evening, and that means very crowded. There might be five people dense on the subway platform. I walked down the stairs and this guy, he pushed people aside and ushered me into the train, and I think that if he had had a cloak or a cape, you know, he would have put it down. He was like Sir Walter Raleigh of Thirty-fourth Street. And I get into the train, and a young man stands up and gives me a seat. And I realized, that's the queen, you know? That's an older woman who they weren't coming on to, they weren't sucking up to, but it was like the recognition of some sort of female power that they liked. That they wanted.

If you feel like you need to be invisible because you're feeling *Oh my God, I'm gonna be sixty,* then you kind of hide yourself. But if you think *I am fifty, I am sixty, I'm gonna be seventy, I'm gonna be eighty, I'm gonna be ninety—and watch out, world, here I am,* I think it's really contagious, and people like that, you know?

THE SPIDER WOMAN
CONNECTS US ALL

In Southwestern Native American mythology, the Spider Woman spun the lines that formed the earth: east, west, north, and south. She then used the clay of the earth to create people, attaching them to threads of her web. This thread was creative wisdom. She sent floods to those who forgot her precious gift, but those who remembered climbed into the womb of Mother Earth to safety.

Patti Hammond-Kovach

Chapel Hill, North Carolina | April 2003

This is actually a new skirt and is the first time that I've ever worn it, but the reason that I wore it is because my mom sent it to me. Actually, most of the clothes that I wear that I really like, including my shoes and stuff, are things that my husband or my family have bought and given to me. They make me feel really powerful because, well, they have good taste, and also because I'm really close to them, and so when I'm wearing things that people whom I love have given to me, it's kind of like carrying them around with me.

I'm an identical twin. And you see me kind of dressed up and with makeup and the blow-dried hair, and this is largely the result of my sister telling me, "Patti, you really could look so much better than you do." My mom and my sister were very concerned about me wearing really baggy, kind of ugly clothes all the time. And the reason they were concerned about it was, when I was fifteen I was raped. For a period of about three years afterward, I went very inside, and I didn't want to wear anything that made me look sexy, and I didn't want to look pretty. I'd

Trappings interview portrait,
the Women's Center

go to family reunions and people would look at me, and they'd be like, "Patti, this is not you." Because before I was raped, I was very outgoing, I was very comfortable with myself in whatever it was that I was doing or wearing. Because I felt so self-conscious, I didn't want to draw any attention to myself.

Part of my becoming more at peace with myself was deciding that I wasn't going to be afraid, because when I was raped it was by somebody that I knew. And yet I had this reaction of being afraid of everybody. Actually, I was raped two more times in college, and they were kind of situations where I had somewhat re-created what had happened the first time. And people who have worked in sexual assault know that survivors will put themselves in situations that are similar sometimes to feel more powerful about it. I went through this whole pe-

riod of being scared, and then I realized, everybody who had ever hurt me were people who I knew, and who I had trusted, and who I had let be close to me. So all of this being safe when you walk out to your car and not wearing high heels and not walking around at night, I was like, *Well, that's bullshit.* I'm not going to worry about that anymore because if something's gonna happen, it's gonna happen. And obviously things have happened already, so I'm just going to live my life and I'm not gonna be afraid. If I want to walk around at night, I'm gonna walk around at night. If I want to wear the skirt, I'm gonna wear the skirt. I like to wear low-cut things sometimes. And you know, now I don't feel scared. I do feel self-conscious, but that's different for me. It's not *I feel like somebody's going to attack me,* it's *Oh no, they're looking at me, what are they thinking?*

My husband worries about

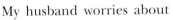

me a lot. I have to just tell him: If you want to be worried about these things, I respect that, but you have to respect that I've decided I'm not going to be scared of some stranger coming up and hurting me, because if you look at it statistically, you're the one who's most likely to hurt me, and I'm not afraid of you either. So that's kind of why—well, that's a lot of why—I've decided that I'm comfortable wearing things like this. So it is an act of love when they send me stuff because they see that I'm out there and not being scared.

I also brought my gym clothes, because I recently lost a lot of weight. I started running, and I never thought that I'd be able to do that. Never. Last month I did my first 5K. I ran almost the whole thing. For me to be able to do that now makes me feel very powerful. I used to be very athletic. I was a black belt in tae kwon do when I was a kid. Being physically powerful never helped me in these other situations, because the people who hurt me were people who I knew and trusted, and who I didn't feel like I could defend myself against because I was so shocked emotionally that they were hurting me. I don't think I'd ever have a problem, like, punching a stranger.

Heather Arnet

Pittsburgh, Pennsylvania | January 2005

T his purple cape is the first thing of luxury that I ever bought for myself. I come from a very working-class family. When I was sixteen, I got to be a congressional page in Washington, which was very exciting, to leave home and live in a dorm with a bunch of other sixteen-year-olds. We actually made a salary. The deal with my parents was that I could do this crazy thing if it cost them no money. So I was a little bit different than some of the other kids that were there, who I don't think were using their paycheck in similar ways. I think for some people it was sort of like allowance.

One day I went with my friends to the Pentagon City Mall and saw this cape. I absolutely fell in love with it. I remember it was fifty-five dollars. I just thought, there was no way, you know, I could spend fifty-five dollars on this thing. So I didn't get it. Then I went back like every week to visit it. And then I came up with this system of putting away a little bit of money for the cape each week. I thought, *Well, if it's there by the time I have the fifty-five dollars, I could go back and get it.* And it was. So I got the cape. I wore it all that year in D.C., and it's gone through all these different life stages with me. I was actually kind of like a goth teenager. I was trying to think back to that in preparation for tonight, *What did sixteen-*

Trappings interview portrait,
Cecile Springer's home

year-old Heather like about this cape? And I think it's 'cause I thought it would go with all of my black clothing. It just always comes in and out of my closet.

Recently, I became the executive director of the Women and Girls Foundation, and it's been a wonderful kind of coming-home experience to take this job, because my great-grandmother was a suffragette. She wasn't anyone famous, she was a woman on the street with a sign. When the suffragette movement was happening in New York, she became involved. My grandmother talked about this very often. Social justice has been a part of our family history. And politics was taken very seriously, sort of the constant dinner conversation topic, or any conversation topic. You couldn't be apathetic about what was going on in this country, certainly, and in the world as well. And my grandmother, I always remember her talking about voting. Whenever I think of her, I always think of her saying, "You have to vote. You have to vote in big and small elections. You have to vote in all of them because your great-grandmother fought for you to have that right. So you don't have the right to disregard it."

Heather's grandmother Vivian Goldstein and great-grandmother Mary Rosenberg

One day I was going back to a book of mine about the suffragette movement, and they wore these purple banners when they stood outside of the White House in particular. It was like this photo recall moment for me. The purple cape now is this sort of memory garment for those women. So when I've gone into these stuffy boardrooms with a whole bunch of men in their suits, I just put on my purple cape and okay, I can go into the Duquesne Club and I'm ready for them. It's been great because I feel so powerful when I put it on. It is my power garment. I put on this purple cape and I'm like Alice Paul and everybody's with me and we just storm in.

So that's why I wanted to wear this cape, but it also is a *cape*. Ever since I was little, Wonder Woman has been this hero for me. Kind of icon. It really started when I was four years old. I was a child actor and I did some television work. One day a production assistant invited me in, and I could go in their toy closet. I went into this big toy closet and ended up coming out with this Wonder Woman book. Not the Lynda Carter seventies version of Wonder Woman, but the comic book version of Wonder Woman from the thirties. It was a collection of all the comic books, in a hardcover book form, and I just adored this thing. I would just sit around and pretend to read it and learn to read using this book. And it was in college that I went back and looked at the book and saw that Gloria Steinem had written the introduction to the book. And I had read that over and over and over and over again.

Wonder Woman for me was really this character about female empowerment. The moral of the stories always would be that she had somehow saved some woman or group of women from a dangerous situation, but then empowered them with the ability to forever be different. There was actually one that ends where all these women have her up on their shoulders, and they're saying, "Thank you, Wonder Woman, thank you for saving us." And she says, "I didn't save you, I've shown you that you can save yourselves."

She was this incredible sort of superhero who didn't have lots of gadgets like some of the others but took this social justice path. When I took this job, someone asked me

Suffragettes in their sashes, including Mrs. W. L. Prendergast, Mrs. W. L. Colt, Doris Stevens, and Alice Paul

during the first few weeks what it was like, and I said, "It's like getting paid to be Wonder Woman." I don't mean that to be that I think I'm some sort of superhero, but in that it's being paid to think about social justice all day long. So, this is also a cape, and I did bring my Wonder Woman t-shirt, because I also felt that I have these things I've incorporated into my adult wear that are sort of like, um, kids' Underoos. I think I try and sort of always have at least one of the sort of superhero elements in my daily wear that make me feel powerful.

I didn't know that young women didn't like the word *feminist* till I got to college. I came from this heritage of people who felt so wonderful about these terms. About the term *liberal*, about the term *feminist*, about the term *crusader*, *activist*. These things were all positive terms. When I got to Carnegie Mellon, the week of freshman orientation they had all the freshmen get under a tent. The dean of student affairs stood up on a platform with a microphone and he said, "Stand up if you're from another country." And then people would stand up. And he said, "Stand up if you're Muslim." And people would stand up. "Stand up if you speak more than three languages." And just all sorts of things that are supposed to show us *Oh, we're so diverse.* And then he sort of stopped for a moment and he said, "Okay, listen up, guys. Stand up if you're a feminist." And I was sitting with all the girls from my floor. I stand up, and I look, and I'm the only one standing up of my row, and I'm the only one standing up in my section, and then I could see, I mean, I could literally count on one hand the number of other women standing up in this tent. And there were thousands of us under the tent. And so for the first time ever, I felt really ashamed and embarrassed for me and for them. And really uncomfortable. Afterward, when I went back to my dorm room, I asked them why they didn't stand up. They started to talk about how they weren't feminists with this kind of cliché language of "I'm not a feminist, I mean, I like men." Or "I'm not a feminist, I don't think I'm better than men." They were using terms to define feminism that weren't in my definition at all. So then I asked them, "Well, like, you want to be a lawyer and you want to be a biomedical researcher and you're an engineer. When you get out of Carnegie Mellon, don't you want to make the same dollar for dollar as the guys you're graduating with, with the same degree?" And they all said, "Well, yeah, what's that have to do with being

Heather going to work
(or to her invisible jet)

a feminist?" I said, "Well, that's what feminism means. It means equal pay for equal work." 'Cause that was actually the definition that I was taught it meant, which is a very kind of ERA kind of definition. I couldn't make it mean that for them.

People in power like to keep power. And I think there's incredible power to words. I think that the more you constrict language of power, and the people behind that language of power, and the ideas of power, and make them mean something different, then you start to create some sort of insidious virus that can corrupt the whole thing. I think that's what's happened with the word *feminist*. So that if young women don't own it, if black women don't own it, if poor women don't own it, if it starts to splinter away from one another, then it all loses power.

I wear the silver bracelet or the cape or what have you to remind me of that fun feeling of being powerful. But it's also the feeling, I think, for women, of being other, and having to remember that we are powerful and that we have made progress, but we are also still very much second class in this country and the world. That part needs to not be forgotten.

Misc. Pippa Garner

Santa Fe, New Mexico | July 2005

I'm Misc. Pippa Garner. I go by M-i-s-c, which is kind of a definition of my self-image at this point. My femininity was store-bought thirteen years ago at a point in which I had gotten kind of stale with my career as an artist.

I very early on started doing work for magazines and evolved a sort of satire on consumerism as my theme, using consumer products and man-made artifacts of my culture as a way of spinning off and creating kind of an absurdity with these things. I've done a lot of that over many years, including several full-size car projects. This was as my previous identity, Philip. I felt that I was kind of repeating myself and also being stereotyped for what I was doing. I did a couple of books in the eighties. One of them was called *The Better Living Catalog*, which was a satire on consumer products. It turned out to be quite popular, and I ended up doing the talk show circuit and creating a character for myself that was kind of a small-town inventor that had come up with all these wonderful new products for a better world that in fact were ridiculous. But the inventor didn't quite realize that. As I say, it was kind of a shtick that I had created inadvertently.

I began to see myself as an artifact. My style, and even the fact that I was Caucasian, you know, as a kind of a symbol of the privileged class in our culture. And I thought, *What can I do?* There's maybe some potential there for satire. So I kinda turned this beam that I had focused on things that were external at myself, and I saw potential for an art project that would be ongoing, that would always create a disorientation in my position in society, and sort of balk any possibility of ever falling into a stereotype again.

I wasn't quite sure what direction this might take or what form it would take. There was a lot of attention in the media at that time on gender. It had possibly evolved from some of the things that had gone on in the seventies and into the eighties, of feminism and other things that made people self-conscious about their gender role. I thought, *Well, you know, this is the cornerstone of identity: male or female.* If you go into a room of people, the first thing you pick up is whether it's predominately masculine or feminine, and you build on that. I think it's more profound than race or any other thing that could be used as a way of making categories for different people. So I thought if I could hack gender, I'd really be onto something because it would alter everything else I did.

At the time I was approaching fifty. That's a time that you kind of reach a point where you start to look for a comfort zone, and settle into something that becomes consistent and reliable and will see you through the rest of your life, which I should have done at that point. But there's some kind of subversive element in my personality that always wants to self-sabotage the minute I become too comfortable with anything. I was also quite masculine, had a strong male sex drive. I was never gay, and so I was pretty stereotypical as a male of my generation.

Trappings interview portrait,
Linda Durham Contemporary Art Gallery

I thought, *What would happen if I just started experimenting with hormones?* That seemed to me a way of trying out gender hacking without having to commit myself too much, because I could always stop if I didn't care for what was happening. So I attempted to get the hormones legally and discovered that doctors were extremely paranoid about malpractice and you just can't walk into a doctor's office and say, "Hey, I want to do a little experimenting here, you know? My artistic license is valid, so you should be able to honor this."

So I ended up finding a tranny-hooker on Hollywood Boulevard one foggy October night. And I convinced her I wasn't a cop, which I did by paying money. She was very nice actually, and took me to her black-market source. I started on a hormone regime, which I maintained for five years from this black-market source. It did something quite profound. It took the edge off of my feeling about myself culturally. It was a de-masculinizing effect, which I found very comfortable. I was no longer obligated to behave the way that I had been behaving for all my life. It was a new opportunity, although I was still identifying as male.

So, after five years, I thought, *If I go legit with this, and go to therapy, and do all the things that are required if you want to legally change your sex, then what would happen? How far could I get?* I had moved to San Francisco and started therapy. I had read several biographies of transsexuals and I knew kind of what the stereotype was for that, mainly to be born in the wrong body and feel, since childhood, that you were the wrong gender, and secretly cross-dress and all that, which I had never done. I never really had any issues about gender, and so I kind of mimicked that and passed with flying colors, and was able to then get the hormones legally. After five years I was convinced that that was my comfort zone and I had no intention of going the other way. I had the surgery in '93, and came out of it, again thinking in the back of my mind this was an art project. On the other hand, I had done something that altered my position in culture drastically.

The idea of being sort of irreverent about the whole thing was part of it for me. It wasn't like this big life-changing thing. In a sense, it's just like a commodity. It only cost me about five thousand dollars to have the two-and-a-half-hour sex-change surgery and seven days in the hospital. For that much money what could I get, a five-year-old Honda or something? It was a way of actually making a purchase of something that I can incorporate into myself, and know that it will never have to be insured or stolen or anything else. I went out and I bought this. You might have to go through a few hoops, but it's all part of the process.

It's an acting role to some extent to study the mannerisms of the other sex, and to figure out how to pass, as they say. The point of this whole project was to enter into something that had a real question mark floating over it, and then let it drift and see where I ended up. And I felt confident enough that I could deal with whatever insecurities came out of that. I've been through a number of other things that made me feel that I can handle this. I'm a Vietnam vet, I'd been through a lot of stuff up to that point. So I just kind of took my hands off the wheel, pardon the automobile analogy, and let the whole thing drift back to where I felt relaxed. That ended up in a position of ambiguity, which I found I liked because one of my themes as an artist is, well, paradox. I always considered myself a kind of juxtaposeur, and here I had found the perfect balance for that. So I've kind of left it there ever since.

But as far as the power look, which is what we're supposed to be talking about, as you might notice I have some tattoos. I never could find a bra that fit, being 6'3½" and athletic. I found this wonderful woman in town here who does very skillful tattooing, and I thought, *Why not employ the technique of trompe l'oeil, fooling the eye, in tattoos?* So I had her tattoo a bra on me, so it's completely comfortable, and it'll last me for the rest of my life. It's funny because one of the issues, I think, with power dressing for both genders, but perhaps more so for women, is to use clothing as a way of kind of looking naked when you're dressed, bringing out certain contours of the body that would be seductive, and using that as a power implement. I've created the opposite; I look dressed when I'm naked. And then I thought, *Well, as long as we've done the bra, I don't want to be half-naked.* So I had her do a G-string also, which wasn't particularly comfortable, but, you know, it's there now. This woman really got into it. And she also did my wooden leg, which was another thing altogether.

I've been run over twice, as a cyclist, and badly injured. The first time they almost couldn't save this leg there was so much damage. When it all got put back together, it looked slightly different than the right one, and much

Pippa in the lowest form of media

straighter. And it kinda looked to me like a wooden leg. I had seen a painting that René Magritte, the Belgian surrealist, had done in the forties of a female torso, nude, that had sections of wood on the different parts. That kinda was in the back of my mind as a really cool thing, and so I went to the lumberyard with my Polaroid and photographed various woods to try to find something, a nice distinct grain and yet didn't look, you know, tacky like plywood. We picked American oak, which I thought was patriotic. And so that's my wooden leg.

So everything I have on is really part of my normal look. I always dress the same from the waist down because of my riding everywhere. I have to have my shoes and my tights. And I always either wear capris or else roll this side up so that the leg is exposed. So it's kind of a constant from the waist down. From the waist up, this is kind of my dressy look.

As an artist, I like to have a little bit of, not necessarily discomfort, but just curiosity and, you know, What the hell is that? I just enjoy that, and that's the way I like to feel when I'm with other people. To be comfortable, but at the same time be a little bit odd. So it isn't as much a pretentious thing as it is just that's where I am. After the surgery, when I came back, talk about creating chaos. And then having to work through that and find some order. I mean, in spite of my sort of intellectualizing the situation, I was still thrown for a loss. I realized they had done this surgery and, you know, changed my gender, and I was legally female. In fact the state of Illinois, where I was born, even reissued a birth certificate that I was born female in 1942, which I think is remarkable. I became aware, I think, of the separation between what is natural, what relates to anatomy and biology, and what is learned behavior.

It's interesting to be in between. If you want to think of a scale, with M over here and F over here, I've moved a few notches. I don't know whether I'll continue to move further in my life. I'm already sixty-three, so it could be that it's kind of reached a static point now. But maybe not. I have no idea. Things can happen that change a person's personal evolution totally drastically.

What I do for daily wear, I like to have something new every day. About three years ago, I got onto this idea of making a new t-shirt every day. I've been so repelled by that whole look of people, they pay to advertise other people's products on their clothes. And I thought, *That's just horrible.* Then I thought, *On the other hand, it's a great way of presenting an image,* because it's near eye level and you're moving so you get to see the reaction, but you get to move past relatively quickly, so there's no need to stop and dwell on it. You get these sound bytes of reaction. I got really attracted to that. I made this t-shirt that said PRAY YOUR BUTT OFF and started wearing that around. I get not only their reaction to me, the way I present myself, but then here's this caption on the front of me, too, which puts another spin on it. That kind of enhanced the whole thing that I was doing.

It became like a daily one-liner. I can't stop. It's become an obsession. I have to go home every night before I go to work—I work at night mostly—and get the iron plugged in and get out the instant letters and put something together. So I brought a few. I have, I think, a total of about five hundred now if you edited down out of many more than that. Sometimes they're controversial and somewhat perhaps in poor taste, and I don't care. Whatever the best thing I came up with that day is what gets printed. I've been doing work for magazines for thirty years. I like the idea of mass media, and this is kind of a local version. Maybe the lowest form of media is the t-shirt. Bumper stickers are in there, but you need a bumper for a bumper sticker, and a t-shirt, all you

WORLD'S MOST FUEL-EFFICIENT CAR!

need is a torso. So I think it's the lowest form of media. This one says DEFAULT MODE PARANOID. There isn't a lot to explain about these. It's just a matter of putting something on that raises the eyebrows.

IT'S ALL GOOD SINCE TV TURNED MY BRAIN TO MUSH. This was kind of a response to my having done a television show in Los Angeles called *Monster Garage*. They get a team of people that are experts in some kind of car work— I make all these human-powered vehicles. They played up the gender thing there, too. It's such a macho environment, and the host of the show, Jesse James, is this biker guy. His whole image is Mr. Macho with the choppers and all that. But we hit it off really great because we're both kind of fringe artists who are working in a sort of commercial way that isn't compatible with the structure of the art world.

There's a place in town called the Atomic Grill, which is open till three o'clock every night. The cops go in there. They're all in uniform and here I am. It's interesting to see how people at first are put off, and then something happens that they find common ground. My regular feature appears every month in *Car and Driver* as Miss Goodwench, which is a pair of satirical drawings I do on the readers' page every month. Several of them had seen that, so once they found that I was, you know, kind of a gearhead, then they deal with these two things: Okay, here is a person that's transgender, and that's kinda hard to relate to, but at the same time, you know, we love cars. I like that kind of situation. There's always a little bit of edge to it, you know?

Every year, I go to Detroit for the press preview of the car show there, which is the biggest one in the world. The men are dressed in suits, and it's a big deal where all the CEOs get up and give a little presentation. I dress in something that's a little bit more conventional, you know, pants and a top, but I'm always given a lot of respect there somehow and there's never any question raised about my gender. I've never seen another transgender person there, at least that I recognize. A lot of those people have followed my work, so they'll come up and say, "We really like your point of view on our industry." So it just becomes a kind of invisible thing there.

I'd sort of like to go around to different places in the world and just try myself out in different cultures and see what the reaction would be. I just think it's really important that we not put anybody at a disadvantage. We all have the same insides. Power can be used to support an agenda that a person has, and it can also be used as kind of a toy, you know, which is an agenda, too, I guess. But to just say, *What if? What if I do this, what will the reaction be?* That's my sense of it. I haven't really ever used power to further my bank account or any kind of personal gain, which means I'm not in a very advantageous position that way. But I just like to think that I have the freedom to experiment. And that, to me, is what power constitutes. Hopefully I've created a situation where I'll be able to retain that indefinitely. Hopefully.

Hot off the press, October 8, 2006

Garrett Ann Wexler

Boston, Massachusetts | October 2005

I'm originally from southern California. I take a great pride in being from southern California and living in New England, and trying to keep that beachy, laid-back, California-girl attitude alive, even though I'm not a particularly big fan of the beach or wearing bathing suits in general.

I work in a contemporary art gallery and studied contemporary art in school. I grew up feeling creative and arty, and I think that influences the way I dress immensely. I generally shop for designer clothing. I've gotten to the point now financially where I feel I'm old enough to shop in like nice department stores, and I'm not embarrassed to go in anymore and ask for what I want. And that's really upped my clothing ante.

I can talk about the outfit that I'm wearing specifically today. I wore this outfit for seven days straight last week to work. The weather changed, I got to put on my winter trousers, and I didn't want to take 'em off. They're soooo comfortable. And so super stylish. I generally wear motorcycle boots or cowboy boots, sort of classic boot types. Very Americana. And my leather belt chain, conceptually designed to be like if you're wearing your boyfriend's clothing, sort of how it doesn't fit you correctly, but is also really cute and can be sort of stylish and conceptual in its own way. So that's sort of what's going on down here. I've a rock and roll t-shirt on that has really bad B.O.—B.O. and old rock and roll t-shirts, also very conceptual. I get a little concerned that the B.O. gets strong sometimes, but you know, you gotta like roll with it. I like clothes that are easy. Easily stylish, easily fierce, and punk rock a little bit. This is definitely a punk rock outfit for me. It's a little punky.

Power from my clothing means feeling comfortable, sexy, stylish, better looking than other people. I generally dress to intimidate. Not in a negative way. People are intimidated by people who wear strong, bold choices, whether it be like stylish or the complete opposite of stylish. I go into a store and I'm dressed like this and I think a lot of people don't necessarily relate to the way that I'm dressed. And that interests me. Um, the friction there, the misunderstanding, it's sort of like their loss and my gain, and that's exciting.

I definitely, specifically, put outfits together to intimidate one of my ex-boyfriend's girlfriends. And it totally worked. I was living in London at the time, and I was working for a fashion show for the university that I was studying with. And she was kind of a punk rocker girl. Lots of black tights, little pointy flat shoes, pencil skirts, little black cowl-neck sweaters, sort of a black bob. And at that time I was sporting bleached blond hair in a mohawk. He'd actually left me for her, and I felt a little vengeful. She was a designer, and I was actually dressing the models. So I put together an outfit where I wore: python black cowboy boots; super-low-slung trousers with a big long gold chain; and I wore a black thong, and you could probably see, I don't know, about four inches of my black thong, there was a lot of ass hangin' out; a little black men's vest; no bra; um, my hair spiked really high up; lots of black eye makeup; and some jewelry. I mean, it was a pretty like casual outfit, but she couldn't stop staring at me the whole time. I didn't like say anything and I didn't like walk up to her, but yeah, I thought that it worked, and I was pretty excited about that. He ended up dumping her, which was fine for him.

I think that men are equally intimidated by the clothing that I wear. You don't have to wear clothing to intimidate men. I mean, you can just be who you are and they're like scared. Women are a little bit different because they know you and they're of the sort of same seed that you are, so you have to be a little more specific about how you intimidate them. I don't want to intimidate women. That's not true. I want to intimidate people in general, but only because I have insecurity about being who I am, specifically trying really hard to be who I am and to fight against the sort of norm. My defense mechanism is to be like, you know, *I look hot and you don't and I'm gonna tell you why.* But that's simply my opinion, and any woman who wants to defend her look to me and have specific reasons about why she's dressed the way she is, I'm all for. I have no problem with women dressing any way they want, I just want them to know why they're doing it.

A message can be crafted through your clothing. I was reading an interesting article that was talking about how women don't dress for their boyfriends, they actually dress for other women. I mean, it's hard to get compliments from women, you know, women are just a tougher audience. That's where I think the intimidation comes from. It comes from the dialogue that I want to have with other women. I want to challenge them, you know? I'm an outgoing, normal girl, and this is how I dress. Like, you're a normal, outgoing girl, why do you dress the way that you dress?

I've always had a huge connection to what I wear, what my friends wear,

Trappings interview portrait, Simmons College

what my family wears, what my partners wear. I dress my entire family: my mother, my sister, my boyfriend. I mean, my boyfriend was a cute dresser when he met me, but he's a fantastic dresser now, and has a full-on conceptualized look from head to toe and has some designer pieces that like, you know, I had to like drag him kicking and screaming to buy. That sort of like organic relationship with fashion's always been a huge part of my life.

Just recently in the last year, I was like, *Maybe you should be a fashion designer. Maybe you can really do it, maybe you've been thinking that you can't do it and that it's for somebody else for a really long time, and that's bullshit, and you should just like get on the horse and deal with it.* I don't like how high design and high fashion is relegated to a small set of body types, zero through eight. I want to teach women how to wear clothing that's flattering to their body and makes them feel good.

Dana Jacobs

Pittsburgh, Pennsylvania | January 2005

I'm eighteen, I'm a senior, and I'm from Philly. I'm goofy and serious at the same time. I'm a Libra, you know?

This outfit makes me feel powerful 'cause it's like I'm ready for anything, you know? For job interviews, and if you go in a store ain't nobody going to watch you like that, you know, they ain't going to follow you or nothing like that. You legit. Like when you go for job interviews and stuff like that, you feel ready, you feel like you got the power.

It's comfortable. They look classy, they look right. I got to look sharp, too, when I'm dressing like this 'cause if you mess it up, you mess the whole dress code up, you out of here. You done messed the whole game up. This place that I'm at right now, they give you practice and tips on how to do job interviews and they make you dress up for it. So you can get prepared and ready to go to a job interview.

All my family, really they all over, like in South Carolina, they in Pittsburgh, too. Virginia, Alaska, all that. My dad Alaskan, Native American. My mom and my dad took me to powwows and Indian centers and everything like that. But I didn't really get into it all like that 'cause I'm from Philly, and in Philly you don't learn stuff like that. I'm more on my mom's side of the family, my mom black.

I went to Alaska one time. I met my grandma. It was nice. She gave me hugs and

Trappings interview portrait, YouthWorks Inc.

kisses, things like that. It was nice, though. I got five brothers and one sister, two sets of twins. I got a twin brother. It was hard having brothers with me because they used to always beat me up—lie to you not. Especially my twin brother.

So that's why I'm rough right now. They ain't going to leave you alone till you start fighting back but, I mean, I thank 'em now, 'cause I need that. I need that. I need strength in school 'cause, you know, when there's trouble in school and, you know, you get into a fight. I don't start fights. I end them. But I don't like fighting for real for real. Let's not talk about that right now. I'm classy.

Iris Scott

Memphis, Tennessee | October 2002

I'm thirtyish, that's all I'm sharing. I'm the assistant director of the Women's Health Initiatives at the Mertie Buckman Branch, but really I work with the babies. That's what I call it. We did a self-esteem workshop this summer for little girls, age seven to eleven, and it was basically like I got paid to play.

I was told to wear the outfit that I felt most powerful in. So these are my Old Navy jeans that I've had forever. As you can see, at the bottom they're nice and soft. I got them when my son was six months old. It was the Gap back then. I was upset because before I had my son I was 90 pounds. When I gave birth I was 140. So I was upset, I thought I was huge back then. These were my fat girl jeans, I thought. But as time changed, I'm like, *Whew, thank you, Lord! I can still fit.* So I've grown into them. I'm comfortable with that now. It took a long time to get there 'cause I thought I was huge when I hit 120. You know, I was dieting and starving myself, and then I had breast cancer two years ago. And it's amazing that when they tell you that magical word, *cancer,* everything else kinda comes into place. And I was like, *Whatever, I'm still here. I got both of 'em,* you know. So we're cool.

I call this my contingency outfit. You never know what is going to happen during the course of a day. I am very spontaneous. Somebody can call me up and say, "Iris, let's go shoot pool." And I'm like, "Okay." You can take this off, have

Trappings interview portrait,
YWCA conference room

85

the sleeveless turtleneck on, take the glasses off, red lipstick—you know, psych a guy out thinking you can't play. Then if I have to be, you know, professional, I can take the black turtleneck off, close the shirt, sit down, and nobody knows you have on jeans. So it's my contingency outfit.

I'm very plain, low maintenance. Low to no maintenance if possible. Really. I'm the mother of a fourteen-year-old, which in itself is a job, so I admire most people who can do this and have multiple children. I commonly say that puberty is going to kill one of us. And you know, I think it's going to be me that folds under. Back then I thought that I had to look just like they did in the magazines, which included the long hair. I had to have the long nails, perfect makeup. You wouldn't catch me dead with glasses on. I had to have my contacts, even got an eye infection from wearing them too long. But at the same time, when I was being Totally Iris, I was plain. This was me. So as I've grown and evolved, I'm still me, but now it's even more so. I figure, you know, if you don't like me with no makeup on, then you don't get the treat of seeing what I really look like when I dress up. You know, because I have a nice figure, but I figure why put it out there every day? It's a treat. If he doesn't take me like this, he doesn't get the treat. That's it.

We are the prize. They have to work for the prize. If you just put it out there unwrapped, nobody values it. You gotta wrap it up nice. And when you're unwrapped, it's like, *Yeah, this sister work out.*

Memphis, Tennessee | March 2006

I'm now the director here at Girls Incorporated, where we encourage girls. Life is good and lots of things have happened. We lost the funding at the Y; I came here to the Girls Incorporated center. I started doing a summer camp, a leadership development camp, which led to me actually taking over this center, which is the largest one. I have eighty-six girls.

I just believe that everybody has their own gifts that the universe gives you. I tried to fight it, but ever since sixteen, seventeen years old I've always ended up working with children. I went back to school and decided to get a degree in psychology, and then in counseling psychology. No plans of working with children, ever. All I wanted to do was wear a nice Gucci suit, nice Manolos. But every time I started working in that area, I might need a little money for something, and then something would pop up with me working with children. So I give up, this is where I'm going to be. With children.

Our mission is to inspire all girls to be strong, smart, and bold. So we work with girls from all walks of life. Girls, no matter what their socioeconomic level is, they suffer from low self-esteem. Even though we had in the seventies Wonder Woman, now you still have girls thinking certain things are girl jobs, boy jobs. What I'm here to do is tell them, "You do anything you want to do." That's what I do, and I love it.

It was told to me that the word *bold* is not acceptable for some because that's a negative word for some women. But here, we use *bold* in all senses of the word. You can be bodacious. Bold also means blazing the path. Just because you don't see a road already there, make one. That's where you want to be, and you know that that's the easiest path for you, make your own path. And my staff are all dedicated to it as well. And then *we're* bold. Some days I might be subdued in what I wear, and other days this is actually what I wear to work. I may feel like wearing this and the bright red lipstick. If you feel bad, put yellow on, you know, wear something pretty. So the girls are kind of getting into that. Even though they have to wear uniforms to school, they will jazz up their uniforms. Some day they might want to wear a sparkly belt— if that's what you feel like wearing, do it. That's part of what we do with bold.

Power to me is influence. Powerful to me is being able to make a phone call, I plant a suggestion, just a little bitty suggestion, and a

Iris at Girls Incorporated

87

couple of days later, "Oh, I had this wonderful idea," and you're like, *Yeah, send it over here.* That's power to me. It's not manipulative, it's influence. It's not what you can do, it's how you can get it done, and my thing is getting it done. And that's Totally Iris. Totally Iris is when I'm thinking three steps ahead. And when it all works out, I'm like, *That's working.* Yeah, that's me.

I tell the staff here that we have to plant the seeds very early. This is my power base, my girls. In twenty years, I want to look up, if something happens and all the utilities go out—like we had an ice storm, only certain sections of the city, you know, got their utilities back on quicker—I want to be able to make a phone call to one of my babies and like, "It's Miss Iris, honey. Miss Iris has no lights. Could you make that happen?" That's what I want, and I want them all placed in positions of power, not the assistant executive director. I want them to be the executive director, I want them to be the chairperson of the board. I want them in all these little positions all over the place.

Women are very powerful. I just bought a t-shirt the other day that said TGIF—THANK GOD I'M FEMALE. And these guys were like, What does that mean? I was like, Well, we can do all kinds of things. You know, look at Hillary Clinton. She's like blazing this path, and a lot of people say she can't be the president, and I'm like, She's already been the president. I mean, Bill told you that, This is your co-president, you got two for one. We're the ones that really think of things, and plant the seeds, we can have babies, we can feed the babies, we can cry, we can stop crying, we just do it all. Being a woman is a wonderful thing. And that's what I want them to know.

Anna Laurenzo

Oxford, Mississippi | October 2002

This is my favorite shirt and my favorite shoes I'm wearing. 'Cause I love, 'cause, I don't know why. Because it's *Star Wars.*

My aunt gave me boys' boxers for my birthday and I'm wearing them. Because they're really comfortable and they're for boys. And I am a tomboy. It's a girl that likes boys' stuff. Boys' light sabers, and the *Star Wars* movies, and my dad's BB gun, except I've never shot it before, and he hasn't shot his BB gun in a long time. He only shot it once, and that once would be when I was a baby.

There isn't any girls' light sabers. They use light sabers on *Star Wars.* Boy characters, they're more clever. They don't do as much bad stuff as the girls do. Because Padmé, she tried to get Jar Jar Binks to stop getting that wiggly thing and then Anakin comes and says, "Hit the nose!"

I do have a NASA suit from my aunt. And it's blue, but she didn't know yellow was my new favorite color. I got really tired of blue. Yellow's my first favorite color, blue's second. And like, if I was a girl, then my favorite color would be purple, like my sister, if I wasn't really a tomboy.

When I was a baby I thought of myself as a girl, then I was a dog, then I was a cat, and then I was a tomboy.

Trappings interview portrait,
Oxford Public Library

I am eight years old and I live in Oxford, Mississippi. When I was four, I told about my *Star Wars* t-shirt and soccer shorts and flip-flops, and so now every time I go to the Internet and type in "Anna Laurenzo" it shows me this tomboy in *Star Wars* t-shirt and soccer shorts. I've heard it a million times and I've almost memorized it, but I haven't heard it in a long time. I feel like it describes me and shows how I was. Well, half of it's changed and half of it hasn't.

If I was going to change back to a girl when I went to a different school, I still had the same friends and everything, they would think I was crazy going from this to this to this to this. We had already bought like six pairs of girl clothes 'cause I thought I was going to do it. And then I wanted to stay a tomboy again, but my mom said, "We already bought too many clothes and so you're gonna have to go as a girl." I'm still a little bit of a tomboy, well, kind of a lotta tomboy still, but I go to school dressed as a girl. I like boys' clothes more, but have to wear girls' clothes. I miss being a tomboy a little and like being a girl a little. My friends still think of me the same, and, well, they're still the same to me. They change a little bit, but they're still the same.

I stopped playing soccer. Now I hate soccer. I did notice it tired me out very easily and it was just kicking a ball around for nothing, and so I decided to play baseball and swim team because I love to swim. I feel like the queen of the water, you know? There's a few strokes that are a little hard, and the races are a little hard. I get nervous before races. I do all this practice three times a week for about four swim races a year. There are a whole lot of races, but my mom doesn't let me do very many. I'm gonna have to talk her into letting me do more. I'm a pretty good briber.

My family plays baseball. My grandfather, my other grandfather, my cousins, and my dad and my brother are big fans of baseball, and I like it better than softball. It's not weird to me because I know all the positions and how to pitch and stuff. And I like a boy who might be on my baseball team. And the bad thing about it, I may be the only girl in the whole baseball league, because baseball's a boy sport and softball's a girl sport. I don't really care. I just like playing baseball 'cause it's fun.

I feel like I rule all the sports, and I really love sports. I'm one of the strongest people in my class, but people still think of me as a boy. It's kind of

Anna in her bedroom

very weird to think of it as super girl, but I don't know, I still have a boys' drum set and a boys' disc flying saucer thing. I do play with dolls though.

You know, there's a whole lot of tomboys out there who want to be boys and there's a whole lot of, well, not a whole lot of, but like a few boys who want to be girls. So I think it would be fair if there was boys' stuff that's unisex stuff in girls' sections, and just a little bit of girls' stuff in boys' sections. I think things should be mixed.

I have lots of power outfits, but this one was just in my closet. I'm wearing my Puma sweatsuit and it looks kind of unisex, but it's got a purple shirt under it and glitter. I define power as, you know, kind of something or the power of the world. You know, you have all and you can control it. What makes you feel like that is a power outfit. It makes you feel like you can do whatever it is. I could do any sport in this outfit. Tennis, baseball, football. Any girls' or boys' sport in this because this is pretty unisex.

Meg Anne McGurk

Chapel Hill, North Carolina | April 2003

When I was about sixteen, my best friend, Jill, who is still my best friend, got her license before me. She also got a car when she turned sixteen. That was the beginning of discovering the rest of the world.

She said, "Meg, we have to go get black lace bras at Victoria's Secret." Had to be Victoria's Secret. And I said okay, and she goes, "Because we are going to be incredibly powerful if we have on black lace bras." So we went and we got them and we rocked. We would ask each other, "Do you have on your bra? I got on my bra." You know, it really did cultivate this incredible sense of power. And I even have on my backup one tonight 'cause I wasn't willing to take off my shirt and stand here in my black lace bra. And of course it has the matching underwear. I believe at all times that I need to be matching, which is difficult to obtain every day, but I manage to do it.

I was thinking about it, and it's kind of, to me, like being a superhero. Like Superman or Supergirl wears their suit underneath their everyday clothing, but when they become the superhero they tear it off. And I can be in any situation, it doesn't matter the outer clothes that I have on, if I'm needing that boost, I feel like I could pull open my shirt and go, "Don't mess with me now. I've got on the black lace bra." And you can't mess with me when I have it on. I am incredibly powerful when I have it on.

Trappings interview portrait,
Street Scene Teen Center

Mary Phelps Jacob was born into a prominent New England family from New Rochelle, New York. She struggled against the social norms of this privileged set for most of her life. "Polly," as she nicknamed herself, was the first to patent the brassiere—a backless model she invented during the season of her social debut in 1910 to free herself from corsets so she could dance in comfort. She lacked the business sense to market her brassiere, though, and ended up selling the patent to Warner Brothers Corset Company for $1,500.

After meeting her second husband, the poet and publisher Harry Crosby, she changed her name to Caresse and moved to Paris. A writer herself, she wrote an autobiography, The Passionate Years, *in addition to volumes of poetry. She also opened an art gallery in Washington, D.C., started an art and literature journal called* Portfolio, *and founded Women Against War, an organization for world peace.*

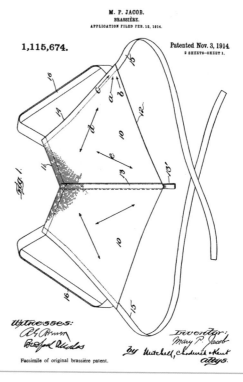

M. P. JACOB.
BRASSIÈRE.
APPLICATION FILED FEB. 12, 1914.

1,115,674.

Patented Nov. 3, 1914.
2 SHEETS—SHEET 1.

Facsimile of original brassiére patent.

Peggy Shumaker

I first came to Alaska in 1985. I did an interview over the telephone and got the job, then threw what I needed into my Honda car and drove up here from Arizona. Drove solo all the way up here. Figured I'd meet interesting people, and that's turned out to be the case.

I think living in Alaska has taught me a whole lot about appearances and how much they don't matter. I'm a writer. I write nonfiction, but mostly poetry. I think one kind of clothing that writers use is words, and sometimes whoever gets to name things gets to determine how they're viewed, and what people think about them, and what they're allowed to be. So I'm gonna tell you a poem, because it's one I can remember because it's funny. It's called "Clitoris."

Surely a man named it.

If a woman had chosen, we'd
have hawk tongue, pearl
of flame, olala berry,
suck nubbin, jujube
tsunami.

So the way we think of things, the way we look at things, often comes through words. Because I'm a writer, I also brought you another piece, which I could not memorize. It's called "Turquoise Dress," and it deals with the topic that we're here to talk about: power, and clothes, and appearances, and assumptions.

Just before I started fourth grade, my mom brought home from a rummage sale a little turquoise dress with puffed sleeves. The fabric, sheer as running water, cascaded over my head and baptized my body. So cool. Like wearing my own personal cloud, in a place where rain's a rare blessing. A black velvet ribbon tied around the waist. Not in back like the

Trappings interview portrait, the Annex Gallery

sashes on little-girl dresses, but in front, a touch of elegance I tied myself. I slid the bow over my left hip.

That year, my teacher Mrs. Garner opened the world of the arts to me, took time away from teaching us the exports of Brazil to have us choreograph our own dances, write and act out our own plays, put down on paper our private songs and stories.

She had as much fun as we did building the Amazon out of chicken wire and papier-mâché. I spent the most time on our life-size crocodile, mixing just the right shades to paint the ivory teeth and jungle-green toenails. When he wasn't there after Christmas vacation, I was sure he had whipped his tail and torpedoed away underwater.

I wore the turquoise dress every day I could get away with it. It was the first garment I learned how to wash out by hand. Hung on a painted wire hanger (I was careful to choose one that wouldn't rust), the dress dried quick as a good laugh.

In the turquoise dress, anything could happen. I could fly to school, arriving for patrol duty before my feet even knew where we were going. I could play my stop sign like a guitar, and sing "Cielito Lindo" to the Catalina Mountains. Loitering at recess by the ramada, I would *look* ordinary, but I could be swimming with manta rays and sharks. Watching the world through my sleeve of water, I could hold my breath as long as I wanted, and live for years under the sea.

Powerful, I could walk home with Karen Pfantz, even though the other girls would make fun of us. Karen wore faded old lady dresses from the bargain bin at the Disabled Vets store. Karen got the lowest grade, always. After every test, she lifted the lid of her desk and let big drops water her notebooks. The popular girls jeered, "You don't like *Karen*, do you?"

"Just ignore them," I told her. She tried. Her horsy face gathered itself up as if she were trying to refuse the bit. We took the long way to her house, playing under the footbridges where they crossed the arroyos, getting a drink out of the Roushes' hose. We wondered out loud if their lives were better in the Roushes' house since Mrs. Roush painted the top half lavender. She left the bottom half bare adobe.

Eventually, though, we had to take Karen home. Her father would rouse himself out of the stupor of that day and growl. I stayed as long as I could, knowing that as long as I was there he wouldn't do to Karen what he did to her every day after school. That turquoise dress made me brave so I could stay. Then I'd go home to see if Mom was drunk or sober.

One day, Karen didn't come to school. Nobody said anything. When I asked, the nurse told me she moved to Florida.

Blessings on you, Karen Pfantz, wherever you are, I thought.

A dust devil swept the playground, and I crouched down so my turquoise dress could shield my bare legs. Red—all I could see with my eyes hidden in the crook of my elbow was red, the waxy tulip shade seen through closed lids. As I stood up after the storm, a stampede of boys headed my way from the tetherball courts. *Ya-Ya, Ya-Ya,* they bellowed. One grabbed my sleeve, hard.

Almost slow motion, how the fabric gave way. Almost an early-morning dream, when you don't know if you're asleep or awake. The sleeve's seam held. Threads all across the back let go quietly, no great rip. Karen, never complaining. My dress hung down over my bare shoulder, my slip strap in plain sight.

Where did they come from, those big gulping sobs? I hardly ever cried, and never in front of people. Even when the bell rang, I couldn't stop. The boy, defending himself before the playground monitor, said, "Why are you so upset? It was an old dress. You wear it every day."

The playground monitor meant to console. "He only does that because he likes you, you know."

I shuffled in, huddled under my desk lid. My cloud had torn. I couldn't mend it.

Mrs. Garner took me aside, murmured, "You don't need a special dress to be powerful. It was just a reminder."

Power means having choices, having options. Power means, um, getting up in the morning and being able to do what you wish to do that day. Power means connecting to those who have gone before, paying attention to those who are alive with us at this moment, and knowing that we're connected to those who won't show up until long after we're dust.

Kim Hafner

Jersey City, New Jersey | October 2004

I guess I'll talk about what makes me feel powerful. For me to feel powerful, I think I have to feel gorgeous. Not beautiful, not pretty, but gorgeous. It doesn't have to be a specific outfit, but lipstick in general is key. I never leave the house without lipstick. All other makeup is optional, but lipstick is a must. I can wear browns or whatever, but if I really want to feel powerful, like today, like being nervous and knowing I had to get up in front of everyone, I wore my red lipstick. My sister went to Paris. She was a lipstick wearer, too. She always said most women think of Parisian women like the height of glamour, but Beth thought that they were missing a little something, which was lipstick. I think women in general look better with lipstick. It kind of brightens you up and makes you feel really good. Maybe because it makes me feel really good and beautiful and sexy. So red lipstick is the key.

Trappings interview portrait,
Jersey City Museum

It's all about your attitude, and you have to have a Red Lipstick Attitude. Even if you have to pretend sometimes that you have a Red Lipstick Attitude when you're not feeling like you have your Red Lipstick Attitude, you kind of put that out there and reach into your like red lipstick little pocket and project that.

Pink to me seems too like frilly, fluffy, girly. Like for me, it's not like a great color. I don't really consider myself so girly 'cause I don't wear nail polish. For me nail polish is like the height of girlyness. I have jewelry on and lip-

Beth and Kim at a wedding

stick, that for me it's not too girly. Nail polish puts you over the edge of girly-ness.

When I have to feel especially powerful, I put certain things on. My sister just died at the end of last year, so a lot of times when I'm feeling really sad and lonely and I need strength, I'll put something of hers on, like this neck-lace. These are two necklaces of hers and she kind of wired them together. I have this ring, which I usually hide under another ring. It's a ring that I gave her right before she went to Paris. It says in French: *Think of me.* So sometimes I feel like if I need strength, I just kind of rub my finger on it.

Even my coat here is actually hers. To me, this is Beth. And I thought Beth was gorgeous and powerful. I feel like even though we were twins, I thought she was the beautiful one. People are like, "But you're identical twins." But she had something in her that I didn't. So when I see this coat, it just makes me think of her, and I felt really powerful coming here because I had stuff of hers.

I realized that my definition of power has changed since she's died. It's like you have these revelations, things you don't really realize until someone that's really important to you is gone. She made me feel really powerful and sure of myself. This year has been really hard for me because I realized I'm not so powerful anymore and I have to redefine that sense of power. Sometimes I feel like I don't know who I am. When she was alive, she was my sense of power because it was such a sure thing for me. Her being there made me okay. And I don't know if most twins feel that way, but I know with Beth and me it was definitely that way. I know that's how I felt. I always thought she was the stronger one.

I think as you get older, you have to realize you have to develop your sense of power in yourself, you know? With Beth dying, I realize I have to now learn how to be alone, be by myself, and no one out there is going to be there for you. You can have friends and family and loved ones, but you at the end are alone. You have to develop your own sense of who you are and what you believe in. When Beth died I thought, *Oh my God, I'm going to be a mess. How can I go on?* But you know, here I am. You have your horrible days where you're crying hysterically in your apartment, and you don't want to get up off the couch, you eat candy, and, you know, you are just miserable. But other days you think, *I can do that.* Sometimes I need little pieces of her with me just so I can say, *Hey, you can do this.* She is with me.

Janine Thibedeau

Fairbanks, Alaska | June 2005

I was born and raised here, and I'm fifty-two years old. On this topic of clothes and power, that is probably the furthest thing from my mind about any given day except for that every once in a while I think, *Man, maybe I better look in the mirror. Do I really wanna go out lookin' like this?*

Then about six years ago I was diagnosed with breast cancer, and all of a sudden I started thinking about clothes. And I remember walking down the streets of Seattle—that's where I did a lot of my treatment—and window-shopping, and seeing the mannequins and the clothes. And I was very attracted to the clothes that were low cut and emphasized that part of our body, and I had a new appreciation for that. Dressing up and emphasizing that feminine part, that is great. I thought to myself, *Oh man, I'm gonna start paying attention to what I wear.* And I was gonna kind of create a new me. Because of other things in my life, I didn't have both the resources financially or time. It just didn't seem really that appropriate. I had four kids at home, and there were a lot of more important things than how I dressed. That I was there was the most important thing at that time.

This winter, I was on a trip with my three sons. A month and a half into my trip, I found out that my house burned down while I was gone. Then came a time when I started thinking about clothes again because I thought, *Well, all I have for clothes are what I have in my little bag right here.* We were thinking about bringing clothes that we could stay warm in on a trip like that. It was all practical, everything was practical. Then my friend and I, we decided we needed some new clothes. Well, I wore this jacket tonight, and this was the thing that I got. I love this jacket. I have to look in the mirror because this jacket is my prized possession in my wardrobe right now.

Everything that I had at that time, I had in the motor home. I had some cooking gear, and sheets and blankets, and some schoolbooks the kids had. If I shipped it home, it would cost so much. And then I thought I'd be having to sort it out. I'd have to say, *Okay, I don't need this, I don't need that.* And I thought, *No, I need it, I need all of this.* So who knows why I exactly made that decision to drive back, but that's kind of empowering to me, to be in a vehicle and being able to drive somewhere. I felt like I was kind of in control.

I feel like I have an inner power and that's Jesus. That's how I get through these things. Sometimes I look and I say: Now, what was my part in this? How come I had divorce, breast cancer, house burning down? People have stuff in their life a lot worse than that. If I can get through those things that I already got through, I can get through this, too.

I got home on Tuesday, just like less than a week ago. And I've been gone for six months, little more maybe. You know, who wants to come back in forty below and try to figure out where you're gonna live? The day I came home, I drove up to my place and several people from my church were already there with shovels and wheelbarrows and a big, huge, forty-by-ten dumpster, and they were already at work cleaning up the ashes. The first two days, I kinda just wandered around. I was like *Yep, okay.* And I looked around at different things that were there. It's interesting what things you find after a fire, that some stuff doesn't burn. A couple of birth certificates were in there. Then I had music everywhere, from one end to the other. Just burned-up sheets of music. That was interesting.

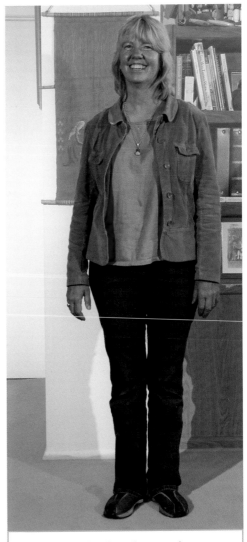

Yesterday in church, I said it was almost fun because it was like a community effort. I mean, we were all there doing that and I had all that help. First couple days I thought, *I'll just turn around and I'll go again. I'll go back to Colorado to my friend's house.* But then I thought, *Well, I could take myself out of it personally just a little bit.* And so I decided I would look at it as if I had just acquired this great piece of property with lots of potential and it was a fixer-upper. And when I get done, then I can sell it or whatever and I'll make some money on it. 'Cause I don't owe anything on it. I owe even less now.

I was going on my own steam for a long time, and I was searching and reading. I was

Trappings interview portrait,
Gianna Drogheo's home

living in Hawaii for several years. My three boys were born there, and my last one was born at home. And that was another empowering thing. I had a midwife and she was a Christian. And I had friends there who were all Christians, and it was something that just kinda meshed at that point—I mean, God spoke to me. And I know that he did because I had a series of dreams, and I thought I had figured out what they were, what they meant. And it was like a big lightbulb went on one day, it was just like the sun came in and brightened up and lightened up everything. It's complicated but it's simple. So that's power. Doesn't mean that I don't run out and go on my own thoughts a lotta times, too, still do that. Yeah, try to figure it out. *Okay, what am I gonna do about my house? Oh no, what am I gonna do? How am I gonna get that place cleaned up?* And I had worry, and I had anxiety, and then I came home and here they all are, you know, helping me do it. So why did I worry? Well, 'cause I'm human.

Towana Welch

I'm a twenty-eight-year-old mother of three. I'm a student at Tennessee Technology Center at Memphis, studying surgical technology. It took me so long to decide what I wanted to do with my life. For a long time I knew that it was something in the medical field, but just being a nurse wasn't enough for me. I wanted to be in on something, in the action, in the midst of the big stuff. So I chose surgical technology.

My job is very important because, number one, I'm the only one in the operating room who can do my job. I'm responsible for setting up, creating, and maintaining a sterile field during all surgical procedures. A lot of you don't know that most of the infections in the surgical suite come from the surgical team. Well, I'm there to try to cut back all of that. Everybody thinks that surgical technologists just pass the instruments and that's it. It entails a whole lot more than that.

This, this is my empowerment suit. This outfit does so much for me because at this point in my life, I'm so proud of myself because it took so much for me to get here. I started school in July. A few months prior to that I was at the lowest point in my life. Was going through a whole lot of everything. I couldn't deal with it on my own, I had to seek help for a number of different things. Had to take antidepressants and medications for anxiety and all of that. At this point in my life, I am just so proud of me, you

Trappings interview portrait,
Metropolitan Inter-Faith Association

know? And I got here on my own. You know, I had a little push from a sister or two saying, "You're so smart. You can do and be anything that you want to be. You know you just gotta go for it." But it was myself that decided, *Okay, enough is enough, no more sittin' around feeling sorry for yourself. You know, you've got three kids, you are what all that they have.* So I knew that I had to get up, get out, and do something, get something. So this is what I choose to be.

This suit here, I go to school in, I will go to clinicals in it, to the hospital, grocery store, laundry, everything I do. This is my power suit right here. It's definitely my power uniform.

Anna Marie Ludwig

Jersey City, New Jersey | November 2001

I am the mother of two grown people. I'm fifty-four years old, and I'm kind of starting a new life all over again. For the first time in thirty years I've been on my own for a little over two and a half years. And while this outfit is not something I would normally walk around in, it was something that was very powerful for me at a very important time.

I wore this to the first Christmas party I went to four months after I became a widow. And that was a real turning point in my life because I never really took myself out like that. I didn't know what I was going to wear. I didn't know if I was going to wear a short dress, a long dress. I found the pantsuit from however long ago, and I said that was perfect, it was just what I needed. So I put that on, and I looked in the closet to see what kind of shoes I was gonna wear. I said, "Ah, these red shoes look fine," and I just popped the red shoes on, not thinking too much about them.

So I got to the party, and as I was standing in line waiting to get up to the bar to get myself a drink, which was probably the first time I had done that in close to thirty years, somebody ran up to me. A woman I had known for years who was also a widow and was, like, bonding with me because we had the same thing going on in our lives, more or less. She ran up to me and said, "I am so glad that you're wearing those red shoes!"

And for a minute I didn't know what she was

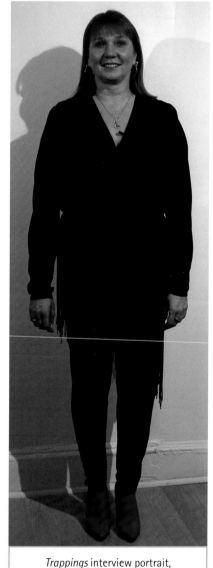

Trappings interview portrait,
Tiffany's studio

talking about. Then I realized that without even thinking about it I picked out the red shoes, which, if you go back to the archetypes, signifies taking back your power. And I realized, *Okay, I am taking back my power, and I need to do that,* and I thought, *All right, Anna Marie! Yeah, you're gonna be okay.*

It was a great party. I danced all night long. I had a wonderful time, and I said, *Yeah, life is gonna be good.* And it has been. It's getting better and better and better. More and more I am taking back my power. I'm learning how to take care of myself, and I'm happy. That's why I chose this as my power outfit today.

Andover, New Jersey | September 2006

This is really cool to be back the second time. Exciting because things have changed enormously. The last time I was kind of just starting out in life. I have since closed the business that my husband and I had started, and I've sold the house that I had. I'm with somebody new now, and we have our own house, and it's a much better place. I've kind of gotten rid of a lot of the old stuff, because I had to become a new person because I was in a whole new space. I don't need those red shoes anymore because the power isn't coming through them. The power is definitely all in me and coming from there. I still have the same power, and even if I'm wearing rags I can still call up the power and be who I need to be when I need to be it.

I work at a coffee shop now, which I've just started doing about a month and a half ago, which is a really big change. This is the cute little apron that I wear. You can see it's authentic because it has stains on it from yesterday's work. I didn't have a chance to wash it. The thing about this job is not the fact that I make coffee for people, it's just the fact that it's a change in life. I was kind of falling into a rut where I was home, and I wasn't really doing anything, and I was just kind of wasting time. And this just kind of makes me feel good. It's fun, and I enjoy seeing the same people coming in every day, and just being cheerful, and letting them have their coffee and then they go. At the end of my shift I walk out and I don't worry about *Oh, did I do a good enough job in that sales pitch that I did?* Or *Is somebody going to come back and have a problem with what I sold them?* Because it's coffee. If they didn't like the cup of coffee, you make them a new cup. So it's fun. I'm feeling good about getting out and doing it.

It was a really big thing for me to go and ask for the job, because I hadn't gone out to look for a job in I guess about thirty-four years. And I walked in and asked for the job and got it. Just like that. I thought that was pretty cool.

This is the other thing that I do, I'm a minister at a metaphysical church. I'm one of about nine ministers. We're all volunteers and we all take turns doing services. It's a really nice church. It's not fire and brimstone, it's just really easy and very accepting.

My husband and I started going together there at the same time. We became ministers in '97. It was a four-year process. You go through classes and you have to do a service, you have to teach classes, you have to head committees, and you have to be consistent and dedicate yourself. You go through an ordination ceremony, you get your robe, and you're given this stole by the church. It's kind of your award of status.

I wouldn't say that this makes me feel powerful. I don't think that's a good place to be in this position anyway. What it does is it makes me feel responsible. It gives me a certain amount of authority when I put on my robe and my stole and I get up there and I'm doing a service or performing a wedding or a funeral or some kind of a ritual type thing. It also reminds you that you have a responsibility, and you need to conduct yourself in a certain way. Even when I'm out of the robes it's changed the way I conduct myself. It's changed the way I think about people and the way I speak to people. I also watch the words I use. I very rarely use any curse words because I think it just reflects back on my po-

The Rev. Anna Marie Ludwig

sition and it reflects on the establishment I'm with. I think that all of us really need to be more careful about that, about how we reflect back on our institution. I also think it makes me relate in a gentler way to people. One of the things that I always go back to is the Golden Rule: Do unto others what you would have others do unto you. I think that this whole thing that I've been doing with the ministry makes me behave more that way than ever before. It's much easier to be happy and pleasant and be nice to people than it is to be mean. Because when you're mean to people, you have to remember who you're mean to, and then maybe you can't be so nice to them. But when you try to be nice to everybody then you can just act that one way.

We are a metaphysical church. Metaphysical really means that which is beyond the physical, and the church really believes that there's more than just this lifetime and there's more to this lifetime. There are many different levels. There's of course the spirit world, and we do a lot of work with the spirit world. We believe that when someone passes over or dies, that's not the end, that life continues, and we can contact those that have passed over. So when our loved ones leave us, they're really not gone. It's very comforting because it doesn't leave that void like, *Oh my God, I'm totally alone.* Well, we're not alone. We're only as far away as a thought or a prayer or just calling out.

That was really helpful to me when my husband died because when I went into the business to start it up again, to run it myself, I walked in and I said, "Hey, I can't do this alone, you got to be here to help me." And I always felt that I was being helped. That he was there helping me and that spirit was helping me.

When I was still married, I was controllable. Now I am more in control. And that's kind of been something I had to do. It's like, *Okay, sink or swim.* So I've learned that I can swim. I am with somebody now, and it took a while to make the transition from having to ask before I did anything to now asking, not permission, but just being respectful. But there's also times when I just say, "Okay, this is what I'm doing," or this is what we're doing, or this is what you're doing. Sometimes I'm told I'm a little bit pushy now, but I think that's kind of in comparison with where I was before.

I feel lightened since the last interview. I didn't know what I was going to do, who I was gonna be. Fortunately, I decided I like the person who I found inside there and who I think I've become, and all that has added to my feeling better about myself, better about my situation, and more in control, and able to do pretty much anything I decide that I want to do. Like, a big thing was going into the city. The only time that I went was with my kids, and it was holding on to their elbows and following. I didn't know where I was going, how I was going to get there, and now I just take myself in and I go. I feel like a real grown-up person now, and it's great because I don't feel like I'm held back. And since I can go there, I feel like I can go anywhere. It's a really great feeling.

The last time you interviewed me, I was taking back my power but it was still a very narrow sphere I was in. I feel, you know, like I've come a long way, baby.

Helen A. Waldorf

Jamaica Plain, Massachusetts | October 2005

I'm an environmental scientist and a member of St. John's Church. Last year I got married, and I never thought that would be possible for me. I hold degrees respectively from Rice, Yale, and Harvard universities and have been fairly well respected in my field. There was the one thing I couldn't do, and the one thing I always felt I had to hide was who I loved. Twenty-five years ago, I met another environmental scientist who I fell in love with and who I married last year. I wore this suit, and it made me feel very powerful getting married, and this is the picture of us dancing.

In terms of clothes, I guess I never really thought about clothes. On the other hand, for a wedding, I wanted to get something special but not too far from what made me feel comfortable at work and effective at work. So this was the compromise. We looked all over town for about two weeks, and finally Judy and I found something appropriate on the second floor of Filene's, not in the basement. We shopped together.

Usually I don't wear makeup either. And a couple friends of mine from work said, "You look really terrific, who did your hair and makeup?" I said, "Hair and makeup by Judith." The times when we've dressed up, we play beauty parlor before we go out. We thought, *What a concept.* We can wear each other's clothes and borrow each other's jewelry, you know? And it's like, many straight

Trappings interview portrait,
Alicia Faxon's home

married couples don't usually do that. Maybe some of them do, I don't know.

But the whole idea of having sort of nothing left to hide, if you will, and everyone getting together for this really blast of a party in St. John's, it was really quite a process. Gay people were just able to get married in Massachusetts, the only state in the country. We set a date so that it wouldn't be so chaotic, right when everybody else was doin' it, but it was close enough to the date that we could plan it and have it at the church. And it was a lovely day, it was one of the most supportive days I've ever had, and that made me feel very powerful.

It didn't occur to me that it would improve our relationship because in some ways, I mean, we're different. Most people don't have a twenty-year-long engagement. I mean, for us, it was like nineteen years when we got married, and we celebrated our real twentieth anniversary this year. On the other hand, it did change our relationship, and it changed my relationship with people at work and with everyone else because now there's, as I said, nothing to hide, and it made me feel very powerful. I actually think it's made me listen more to people when they talk about their relationships, or their marriage being on the rocks, or talking about thinking about getting married for people that aren't married, and what a serious thing it is, and yet what a fun thing it is.

I'll tell you about the proposal. There was a demonstration against gay marriage out on the common, and it was February, it was really, really cold, and we were freezing our hands and fingers off. We're all sitting there singing and everybody's trying to sing and keep warm. At one point I said, "Judy, why are we doing this?" And she looked at me, and we both said in unison, "Because we want to get married." Two people turned around from the church, and they're clapping. And so that was the first time we really talked about it.

When I start talking about it, people start telling me about their wedding and their marriage and their relationship, and it was very interesting 'cause that brought people out to me, and things that I didn't know about other people that we knew. And that was just so wonderful, because it was sort of like, you know, paying it forward. We felt good, it made other people feel good. Then there are people in the country it doesn't make feel so good, apparently, but, you know, they didn't come to our wedding.

This gave people an opportunity to do something that was socially acceptable, you know? "Oh, yeah, I'm going to a wedding, it's my first gay wedding I've ever been to." So that's the way people were talking about it. I said, "Hey, that's okay with me," you know? One of my best friends said it best when she said, "You know, you have an opportunity to live history. Very few people get to do that and know that they're doing that." And I thought that that was probably the wisest thing that I heard that day.

I never thought about it much just because it was sort of like, *Gee, Helen, would you like to take a trip to the moon?* It was a ridiculous question. It was a whole 'nother story, getting Mother to accept this. She didn't come to the wedding, by the way, but she did say the magic words, "You have my blessing." She's eighty-seven and I think it was more of a physical constraint for her. I think it has helped improve the relationship with my mother and it's helped improve the relationship between my mother and Judy. I think very positive energy has been released rather than the negative energy of, like, being held in about ready to explode.

Marriage was made accessible to everyone in Massachusetts on May 17, 2004. In the first two years, more than 8,100 gay and lesbian couples tied the knot. In comparison, more than 36,000 heterosexual couples are married each year in Massachusetts.

There's a lot of positive energy that I think's being released as we speak. It used to be if you were gay, you hung out in bars and it was dark. And bars are not very healthy places to meet people. It's a much more positive, constructive life now that I lead than when I was younger. I think it's giving an opportunity to meet people in a healthy environment. It's good to meet people at work, and at school, and church. And I think this is giving opportunity to young people to, you know, if they are gay they don't feel like they have to hide.

And, by the way, power. I don't think you have to feel guilty about exerting power over someone, because I think of power in the scientific sense, which is work being done to push electrons over time and distance, measured in what we do in my business, kilowatt-hours. And power is the ability to have something that can generate that electricity and push it through distance and time. So it's not over someone, it is a useful commodity. And if we didn't have it, life would be very different. I think of power that way.

Lorraine O'Grady

Brooklyn, New York | October 2005

In some ways we are products of the environment that we've made. I'm in a stage of transition. I may still be searching for the power, or searching for the various amalgams of power. I don't think I'll ever find one kind of thing that will make me feel powerful, but sort of like an array of things that you go through from day to day, week to week, that you feel make you feel powerful.

In this process of aging, and having to find a new style that works, not that's appropriate but that works, I have gone back to the world that I originally came from: the black bourgeoisie world. For my mother, style was everything. I don't know that there was very much else to my mother than style. My mother had been chosen the best-dressed black woman in Boston, and it was something that she took pretty seriously. And when I think about it, it was something that she was training me in from before I could do anything. I remember being two or three years old and going with my mother to Filene's Basement, the original one, and watching her expressions as she found things, and how proud she would be that she had gotten this thing from Bergdorf Goodman's or this thing from Lord and Taylor's, or whatever it was, for this kitchen change. So fashion always had to do with putting one over, getting a bargain.

When I became an artist, and I left the whole world behind that I had come from, part of what I left behind was obsession with style and the amount of psychic energy and the amount of time and so forth that went into it. I have to be kind to the people like my mother and my aunts. I've seen studies that the further away you are from the norm of beauty, the more important beauty is. And so for black people in general, style is a way of bridging the gap between what they are and what the desirable norm is. When my mother bridged the gap, that freed me from having to do it. For me looking good meant spending very little money, very little time, and very little energy. I can't say that I ever stopped thinking about clothes in a very self-conscious way, but it was all geared to freeing me for other things.

I had always, even from the time I was a teenager, worn black. It was just a plus to come to New York where it was the thing to do. I've noticed that the black outfit that I wore at forty didn't work at fifty, and the one that worked at fifty didn't work at sixty, and that's the way it goes.

Power to me is what works. Power to me is what enables the exchange between oneself and the other. However you define the other, whether it's that crowd that you walk through on the street, or that individual person, or that group of people that you may be addressing in the room. Power isn't really just for the self. Power for me also has to do with the effect on the other. And what works now is something which enables me to be minimally invisible.

I don't like the feeling of invisibility. As a black person, one is involuntarily invisible most of the time. Power does have to do with visibility. And it's not just blackness, it's femaleness, it's aging, it's that loss of power as you age. As I've aged, I've become less powerful. Less powerful as a woman, less powerful as an artist, less powerful as just about anything you can name. I'm finding that I have become a powerful person, but for my power to be read, to be accepted and interacted with, I have to tone down my power. The skirt softens it and makes it readable. People's eyes will at least relax on me. They won't just turn away. So softening my power has become one of the key ingredients for me of being able to express my power.

The way I'm dressed right now has a lot to do with having looked at women who have been able to express power. Within the American context, the most powerful form of female dressing that I think we as women have evolved has been the form of dressing of the western woman. I think that this was a woman who had to do it all at once. She had to be able to be feminine and to immediately jump out of the kitchen and onto a horse. I ride a bike, and I can actually ride a bike wearing this.

Trappings interview portrait, Martha Wilson's home

Western women had solved the contradiction of being feminine and powerful in a single kind of outfit. My second husband was a seventh-generation Texan. His father was an official of the Houston Fat Stock and Rodeo Show. So going to rodeos sort of became a thing that I did, and I really noticed the clothing. I discovered that these great things were like as couturier defined as any Parisian clothing that you could find, and as expensive. I realized, you know, it's not just the prairie skirt, right?

I didn't start wearing western clothing until after I got the boots. These boots come from the estate of a friend of a friend. They're custom made. Cost several thousands of dollars. I wore them actually to Chicago and visited that second husband, and when he saw these boots, he said, "God, will ya look at the setback on those heels!" These are some fancy boots. But I have to tell you that the thing that's hottest about these boots is, as I said, I got them from the estate of a friend of a friend, and I heard the story, I didn't know the man who wore these boots, but I heard the essential fact, and that was that he had a seventeen-pound penis. I mean, this guy was into the heaviest of, you know, leather, and he had had some very serious penile implants. When you buy these things secondhand you are getting unknown forms of power.

I absolutely have to have something that reads intentionality. Look, I have never ever stopped being Lena O'Grady's daughter. You know? I really do like to look good. I don't want to go out looking like I just didn't comb my hair. I was forty before I knew what my hair looked like unstraightened. I didn't become an artist until I was in my forties, and it was that process that said good-bye to straightened hair.

I have much more presence this way. People notice me more, and I get much more of a response to me as a fully embodied, sexual being. Not just as a brain. That can be a problem for me, you know, that I can be sometimes too much of a brain or only brain. Whereas this kind of like adds body. The body of my hair adds body. As I walk down the street, I'll notice that guys will see me like at a distance, and they'll be coming on strong. Then I'll come up closer and they'll see how old I am, and they'll be ooh slightly embarrassed and they'll start to look away. But sometimes they won't even get it then.

The thing that my mother would say that was the biggest compliment she could give me, or my sister, or anybody, was, "Oh, that really looks different." She always had this like box of gorgeousness which was handed out by various clothing designers and magazines. But within that, she understood that you had to strive to stand out and to be different. The exercise of personal taste was to not slavishly copy but to introduce your own sensibility. She didn't go the next step from being a follower at the highest level to being a leader, really. That was a step that I could take. So I don't care that other black women of my generation or of my class don't do this. I have gone to a very fancy black event and if I look like this, maybe next month a few of you will have the courage to do what I'm doing. You know, I don't mind being the first one. I don't mind leading in that way. But the corollary is that I don't mind going back to her. I don't mind fitting in. And that I think is a relaxation that comes with age.

New York, New York | October 2006

I had been rethinking the issue of power and the way I had described it in my original interview, realizing that in fact power was not something that was relevant to your immediate environment, but was something that came into play when you took yourself out of your environment. And so there are different ways of going out of your environment. I live below Fourteenth Street. When I ride my bicycle, I can go as fancy as I want because I'm safe on the bicycle. When you're on a bicycle, nobody is interfering with you. You are not really interacting with anybody.

If I'm dealing with a situation where I'm trying to present myself professionally, that's one kind of thing. When I'm trying to present myself socially, there's a difference between just being social and presenting yourself socially,

"It's complicated."

and so the opening, which is part of what we do as artists, that's a presentational mode, whereas if you're just invited to a party, or you're going to a meeting of an organization that you belong to, you're being social, but you're not presenting yourself socially.

If I'm going to an organizational meeting or to a friend's house, but it's a

little further and I have to take the subway, then I'll go into a much tougher street mode. But if I have to take the subway to a place where I also have to be presentational, then I have to be both tough and presentational, you know?

It's complicated. Then if I'm going out to be professional, if I have to like meet a curator, interview with a gallery, or something like that, then I am into a very different kind of presentation. And I'm also into springing the money for a cab. So I'm not altogether about toughness at that point, I'm about like looking like I can take care of business. I think that going to take care of business is not exactly power-suiting, but it's like the art world equivalent of power-suiting.

Those three or four occasions, I do leather at some point. No leather when I'm doing family, okay? I have also tried to simplify life by only having about three or four looks. And one of the looks that I've discovered that really works whether dressing up or dressing down is the Japanese haori, the kimono jacket. Silk and drapey, it really works for very dressy occasions, especially for family occasions, because of the construction. It's not constructed, it's draped, and it's expensive looking. And with everything, jewelry becomes very important because since I've simplified everything, I have to then distinguish, and the way I distinguish is the jewelry. I think in terms of dressing, probably the most difficult and psychically traumatic thing that you can do with clothing is to try to face your family when you've grown apart from them.

Tara A. McComb

Pittsburgh, Pennsylvania | June 2004

I really don't believe in the word *powerful*. What is power? There's no such thing as power, it's all what you think other people think. I've been in Pittsburgh four years, and when I first moved here, I didn't have not one friend. Not one. People would see what I was wearing, what I was driving, and all of a sudden everyone wanted to be my friend because I had Chanel in my hand and Prada on my feet. So I don't believe in the word *power*, because power is what other people think it is. It's a figment of their imagination. But you wanted to know what I wear that makes me *feel* powerful: short skirts and high heels.

I'm thirty-three. I've been in banking for twelve years. And I'm not your typical banker. I'm dressed like this because I love to be dressed like this and have people not pay attention to me, and all of a sudden I'll meet a cute guy at the end of the bar, and I'll let them know that back in the day I was a punk rocker. I slam danced. I followed the Ramones, Dead Kennedys. And you know what, my past, I love it. To me, that's power. Being dressed like that at CBGB's down at the Bowery. My sister sent me a picture. She goes, "Tara, you have a Ramones shirt and Gucci." 'Cause—that's the family. I came from a family that liked to look good. And God

Trappings interview portrait,
Tara's home

bless them, knock on wood, they're beautiful people. They have the best taste. I was going with the other crowd, but I still had the Gucci.

I resented my parents for a very long time. I decided I was going to go to college, and my father said, "Why am I going to send you to school? You're not college material." He said, "Go learn how to do nails." Now, believe me, I love my father. He didn't know any better. My parents were only twenty-one years old when they had me. Irish, Italian, Catholic. My grandmother, may she rest in peace, she lent me the money to go to college. Needless to say I never finished, but anyway. That first year I was working and my income tax came back. So I said, "Nanny, here's the nine hundred dollars that I borrowed." That's all it was. And she said, "Tara," she goes, "you know what?" She goes, "I'm gonna go buy you a full-length fur coat." She says, "Because that's going to take you further." We went. They bought me, eighteen years old, a full-length fur coat, and you know what? You may not like this: For a couple of years after, I felt a little resentment because they were telling me my looks and the way I appear and everything else was going to take me further, and I used to say, *I'm going to prove them wrong, that's not it.* I hate to admit it. They were right. They were right.

Slam dancing in stilettos

I'm not articulate, I'm not intelligent. At the end of the day, that fur coat did take me further than the college education would've. Now some of my very good friends, they're attorneys, doctors, they're this, they're that. And you know what? It's the common sense, the things that my grandmother and my mother taught me. And that fur coat did make a difference. I do have that fur coat, it's a raccoon, it has my initials. I'll never ever get rid of it.

I love to wow people. People look at me and they'd undermine my intelligence. People look at me and they look at my girlfriends, how pretty every one of them are, right? Would you think there was a banker amongst them? That's something that bothers me. Other people's perception that we're pretty, we're cute, we must not have a mind. But you know, we do.

People used to say, "Where'd you go to school?" I'd say "Betty Ford." Just to be a wiseass. What difference does it make where I went to school? Are we in the same place? Are we doing the same thing? Do we have the same friends? Does it really matter? What my mother and my grandmother gave me, the best education in the world can't give you. So I would do exactly what my mother did and my grandmother. And then some. I wouldn't change a thing, I'd just add to it.

Tara with her grandmother and mother

Rocio Aranda-Alvarado

Jersey City, New Jersey | October 2004

This is the kind of outfit I wear when I go to a party. I realized as I was gathering the objects and things I wanted to talk about, there are really two sources of these objects: gifts from women who I admire or who are very dear to me, or objects that were used by women that I've gotten from vintage stores. My shoes and my Jordache fake fur jacket are from a thrift store in Maryland close to where I went to college. And I couldn't resist the shoes because they were so shiny and glittery and I think that glitter is really empowering. I feel powerful when I'm wearing glitter. I think the reason that an outfit like this makes me feel comfortable is in a way it covers me up, because I have body issues. A coat like this covers it all up and it looks fabulous at the same time. I feel like Linda Evans from *Dynasty*.

I'm a curator at the Jersey City Museum. When I'm at work I generally wear a suit. Especially meeting with corporate people who we would like to become members of the

Trappings interview portrait,
Jersey City Museum

museum. Sometimes I put things on so that they can almost be armor. For example, when I go to a scholarly conference and I have to give a paper, I wear my hair slicked back and I wear my glasses and my suit so that I can feel like I'm a serious academic. I don't care about glitter. I'm an academic, you know?

My shoes become my power icon. I have a whole bag here. These were given to me by my sister, and they're the kind of thing that you can't really walk in, but they're great because they're like a sculpture. They're so beautiful. She bought them at a trade show in Las Vegas. She's always been incredibly generous with me. She's a person who I think is very brave; she takes a lot of risks in her personal life and in her business life, too, and I admire her for that. She used to be a beauty editor at *Latina* magazine, and she wrote this article that was kind of about me, actually. It made me feel really good how women who are good at what they do or who accomplished a lot in their life can still wear lip gloss and glittery shoes.

I was born in Chile. I remember growing up I'd be so shocked when people would say, "Oh my God, I have to go to my grandmother's house, I hate it." That's something that I longed for, to be able to go visit family. We never had anybody around. They were all three thousand miles away. We only saw them every few years.

I was lucky because I had a cousin that came to visit and she filmed one of the openings and took this film back to my family. I gave a tour and so she filmed that, too. In that culture, you have to study medicine, law, or business or you'll just never make a living. I feel so lucky to live in this country where you can actually make a living doing what I do, you know? So I think they think what I do is interesting, even though they may not understand it. I send them reviews in the newspaper of shows that we've put on here, and so they love that.

I think power comes from being able to make your own decisions and be at peace with those decisions. Independence is a huge part of having power. When I was little, my Barbie, she didn't have a Ken. She was a single woman, she had a career—and it wasn't as a model, either. She never

Rocio in a shawl crocheted by her grandmother

Rocio and Mary Tompkin, making plans
for their life in New York City

ever was interested in getting married or having a family. What went along with that fantasy was thinking about living independently and making your own decisions. And so that for me is power.

When I was ten my best friend and I thought, *Okay, we're going to move to New York.* We were going to be flight attendants, and then on the side we'd work at the Bloomingdale's makeup counter. That was the dream, we really had it all planned out. We'd be roommates and everything was going to be perfect. I feel like I really achieved a lot of things that I wanted to in terms of being independent and being happy in what I do in my life, so I feel really fulfilled.

Mary Faulkner

Jeans. That's one of my power fabrics. I think that they have spiritual implications. I always feel comfortable in jeans. I feel comfortable in natural fabrics. And height works for me, so I have on these boots tonight. I grew up in Minneapolis, a lot of Scandinavian people and tall, blond women with long legs. It was a disappointing day when I was about eleven or twelve and I realized that I would not grow up to be one of them. I did something about the blond, and I increased the height with the boots.

I'm able to wear anything I want. I work outside the systems, so I can dress the way I want to. Comfort and power probably go together for me, because I can't maintain a sense of being powerful when I'm real uncomfortable. I write. And I can't sit at my computer, I can't write, I can't compose, I can't think when I'm uncomfortable. I'm also a counselor, a therapist. I feel like the real power in that is me not needing to pay any attention to me, and being able to totally plug into the other person. And so in order to do that, I've gotta be comfortable.

I've got one other little thing that I add with the powers. The thing that I'm gonna bring out comes and goes as far as the fashion magazines say. But I believe in them. I carry my shoulder pads. You can't have too many nor can they be too funny looking. Every now and then when you drop one, everyone thinks it's a falsie.

Now I want you to see—I'm fairly powerful

Trappings interview portrait,
Elizabeth D. M. Wise's home

A few prize shoulder pads from Mary's collection

now, right? Watch the buildup of power. I'm getting taller, smaller. Not everybody can pull this off. Now, see how I'm changing right before your eyes. I'm turning into a Modigliani painting right in front of your eyes. I feel like it just creates a spatial relationship that I win. I don't know exactly how, but I look in the mirror and know that I've won.

I have been known to camp in them, to wear them to bed at night when I'm camping in a t-shirt. I'm crawling around with my flashlight, *Where are my shoulder pads?* I may have been influenced by the Joan Crawford era when I was growing up, and you know, that's all about shoulders and power. Those were powerful movies.

Liz Claiborne came out with them already in all her clothes, Velcroed in.

And as I wore the clothes out or passed them along for one reason or another, I would take the shoulder pads and keep them. So I have a lot of Liz Claiborne shoulder pads with Velcro. Thousands, thousands. I would generally probably wear just one set, but when I was pulling this together for tonight I thought, *Why not two?* You know, we're talking power. I don't have to hide it.

Do you laugh at hoop skirts? What parts of your body have you modified? Check if you have:

❏ *Hair: Permed, straightened, colored, waxed, tweezed, lasered, or shaved*

❏ *Skin: Tanned, lightened, bronzed, tattooed, or pierced*

❏ *Breasts: Reduced, enlarged, or padded*

❏ *Waist, Hips, and Thighs: Padded, cinched, or liposuctioned*

❏ *Odor: Deodorized, perfumed, or douched*

❏ *Face: Botoxed, nose-jobbed, tucked, lifted, or painted*

Suzanne H. Bertolett

Durham, North Carolina | March 2002

I'm a law student at the University of North Carolina at Chapel Hill. I worked for a few years before going back to school, and this past fall I just went through the whirlwind interviewing. This is one of the outfits that I wore for my law school interviews, even though technically the women were instructed not to wear pantsuits to their interviews. We were supposed to wear skirts and jackets, but a lot of us just said to hell with that, because I just felt better wearing this than wearing a skirt. I felt a lot less self-conscious in this outfit than I did when I was wearing a skirt. When wearing a skirt I just felt goofier. I had to worry about is it hitching up, is it straight?

So I like this, I think I feel sexy in it. Not because it's overtly sexual—there's nothing that, you know, is accentuated. It's been altered to fit me. Whenever I wear it, I walk a little taller, my head's up a little bit more, and I feel like I'm taken seriously.

My first year of law school, an e-mail went around from career services that said: It has come to our attention that some of the women are wearing pantsuits to your interviews and this is really not appropriate, and we can't tell you what to wear, but you're taking a risk by wearing a pantsuit. And then a lot of people just got all up in arms about it. A lot of people felt offended by it. I didn't feel offended by it. I understood that maybe the safest thing to do would be to wear the skirt and be a

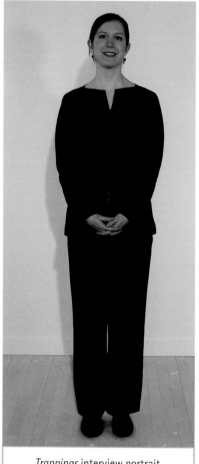

Trappings interview portrait,
Renee's studio

conformist, but I also figured if I wear this and somebody does not want me to work for them because I wore it, I'm probably better off not interviewing at that firm or not accepting a job with them anyway.

In fact, I wore this down to Atlanta, where I went on several interviews, and I got a job offer from every single firm that I have actually worn the suit for. I usually wear my hair slicked back in a low ponytail, to just kind of complete the look. It's almost a masculine look, but it's feminine enough with the way the suit is cut where I don't look like I'm trying to be a man. I just feel like I'm presenting myself on my own terms and not on how other people expect me to look.

Before I went to law school, I was at a job where I just never felt like I fit in exactly. It was very much kind of like a good ol' boy network, you know, everybody's daddy knew everybody's daddy, and they all were these kind of frat boys, and I had to dress a certain way, and was treated with a lack of respect. It was actually one of the things that made me decide to go back to law school, because I was thinking to myself, *I'm so much more intelligent than these people, why are they making more money than I am?* Unfortunately, money is power, too.

I'm thirty-one. I want to have a child sometime, but now I don't know when. I'm going to be close to thirty-three when I graduate from law school. I'm going to be the breadwinner, which is something else that my husband and I are kind of dealing with right now. I tell him I can't get rid of him because I'd be paying him alimony. I can't see now having a child before I'm thirty-five, just because it wouldn't make sense for me to have a baby right after law school when I'm going to be the breadwinner. And that opens up a whole 'nother can of worms: Who's going to take care of the baby? Are we going to get a nanny, or is my husband going to be a stay-at-home dad?

Atlanta, Georgia | July 2004

I am thirty-three years old, and I graduated a year ago last May from law school, and I am now working at a large law firm in Atlanta. I started working last September, and unexpectedly I found out in February of 2004 that I was pregnant. It was very unexpected. I didn't know if I wanted to have children or not—my husband and I thought that we might in the future, but we kept putting it off. It was very surprising to us, but now we're very happy and very excited. It certainly has changed our perspective about who we are and what we want out of life, and has changed my perspective somewhat about what I want out of a career as well.

I find myself less anxious about my job because before I was pregnant, I pretty much identified myself by my work, and my self-esteem was very heavily tied into how I did at my job, how well I felt I was doing, and how I thought other people perceived me. Now I feel like there's this whole other aspect to my life that really balances it out, and I'm able to leave work at the office much more effectively than beforehand. As far as me and Adam, I think it's brought us closer together. We were married ten years before I got pregnant. It's something that we're doing together instead of having these separate lives

Suzanne pregnant and preparing for work

and separate jobs and separate identities. I'm glad to finally be settled in my life, and I guess just having the baby is another way of establishing that.

Everybody at my firm has been very supportive. At first I was going to just take three months off because that would be the paid portion of my maternity leave. And I did some soul-searching, and I just started to get really stressed about the thought of going back to work after three months. I knew I would be traveling. I just found the prospect of having to be away for a few days at a time while still trying to breast-feed a three-month-old baby very stressful, so I decided to go ahead and tell everybody that I was planning to take the maximum, which is six months off. I feel deep down that that's the right decision for me.

One of the secretaries at the office said that she thought I looked very sexy in this dress, and it made me feel wonderful. This is my power maternity dress. I like that it's kind of clingy. I feel better when I'm actually wearing clingier stuff than when I wear the big drapey things. Now that I'm pregnant, I'm in this secret club. I guess that people who have had children really do look out for each other. And one of my dearest friends, she was the first person I told, she brought me in a lot of her maternity clothes, and I wear them quite frequently. Then another co-worker, she brought in probably about fifty items of clothing for me. All these women have wonderful taste, and I feel the best dressed that I've ever felt because of that. I now have more maternity clothes right now than any other type of clothing. Right before I got pregnant, I was pretty much in the best shape that I've ever been in, and suddenly you're just out of control of your body, especially early on. You're so tired. I didn't have the energy to exercise for probably about three months. I've gained at least thirty pounds since I've become pregnant. I still have about two and a half months to go. I feel good about how I look despite the varicose veins in my legs and my spreading rear end. I'm enjoying being pregnant right now, and I think—my opinion may change once October rolls around, but I think I'll probably miss being pregnant.

Once I have the baby, the child's going to come first. How supportive will the firm be when I have to take days off when he's sick? Especially since he's gonna be in day care, he's gonna get sick a lot, it's just a fact of life. I worry about having time for myself. I worry about not being able to keep up at work or just not being happy working full-time. I think those first six months it will be very important for me to be at home, but after that I don't think I'd be happy just being a full-time stay-at-home mom, but I wonder where the happy medium is. And unfortunately, although I love my condo, and I love where we live, the flip side of that is I don't really have the option right now financially to reduce my workload. Ideally, Adam would stay home and take care of the baby, but I don't think he would be very happy doing that right now. So I do wonder where I'm gonna be a year from now, if I'm just gonna be frazzled and miserable or if somehow there's a happy medium or a way to strike a balance somewhere.

Atlanta, Georgia | September 2006

I believe last time you guys interviewed me I was about six months pregnant. Since then, on October 9, 2004, I had my son, Cian. He was about a week early, so I had not even packed my bag. I had planned to take about a week off before my due date. So October 8 was my final day at work. I spent the day just kind of cleaning up files and tying up loose ends. And I didn't feel well the entire day, but it didn't occur to me that I might just be in early labor.

My life has never been the same. It turned my life upside down. He's wonderful now, but it was a nightmare at first. When I got home I was crying. I told Adam, "I want my life back." Cian wasn't eating correctly, couldn't figure how to latch on to breast-feed. And nobody really talks to you about problems with breast-feeding, so I felt like a failure. Time when I really needed to be sleeping, I was taking him to the doctor's office.

The first or second night we had him home, he was still very jaundiced, and they were very concerned. They said, "You need to go to the hospital and have his blood taken." It's about ten o'clock at night. I'm just dead, and we go to the hospital and we have no idea where we're supposed to go. We finally go into the emergency room, and I just have a breakdown. I just start sobbing. I think I was wearing this outfit, this exact outfit. My breasts are leaking, so I have big wet blotches on my breasts, and the people at the hospital were wonderful. They took me and said, "We're not gonna have this newborn baby around all these sick people." So they took me in, like, I guess a little chapel. And they just let me be hysterical there.

I didn't really feel normal again really until he was about six months old. And so really the first six months I was back at work, I was getting up several times at night, then having to be semifunctional at work and just absolutely miserable. And now I can't imagine my life without him. I can't imagine what I did with that free time I had. Wasn't my life empty? I seemed like I was a very happy person back then.

So that's kinda where I am now. I'm still working full-time as an attorney, which is much more than a forty-hour week. I'm seriously considering reducing my hours. My law firm has a wonderful program. You can cut back your hours proportionally, and then take a proportional cut of pay. I'm considering doing 80 percent. It would basically allow me to work a nine-to-six schedule, but then still be allowed to take some vacation, not have to make up time if I get sick, or if Cian gets sick. And even, maybe, take a couple, you know, every now and again, take a day off and just not tell anybody. Not even Adam. Just take some time off and have a day for myself.

Overall, I'm extremely happy. I just feel so blessed. I just wonder why I am so fortunate in my life, but I'm tired. It's interesting that I'm the primary breadwinner in our home, even though Adam does bring home a substantial amount. I still feel like I still have the more traditional, domestic role. Although Adam is wonderful, if I ask him to do something, he will do it, it won't occur to him to do it himself. But he's wonderful. If I say, Adam, could you

clean the kitchen, can you scoop the litter, um, can you change his diaper, he'll do it. But sometimes I think, *Gosh, it'd be nice if it just occurred to him to do it.* Or Adam, will you fix his dinner?—meaning will you fix his dinner, put him in there, strap him in, sit next to him while he eats, clean him up after his dinner, clean up the kitchen after his dinner? But he hears: Fix his dinner.

But I feel very blessed, 'cause he's a wonderful father to Cian and does do a lot around the house. And he is the person who picks Cian up and drops him off at day care. He has to be, 'cause he has the more regular hours. And somebody has to. We have to know that somebody can pick him up at a certain time, and that he won't be there at seven thirty at night with the police.

I would be totally fine if Adam decided he wanted to be a stay-at-home dad. That would actually probably make life a lot easier. They both enjoy being around me a lot, and I enjoy being around them. And sometimes he can't understand when, if Cian goes down for a nap or something, why I just want to be by myself. Not interested in romance, you know? Can I please read a book?

Even now when Cian cries and cries and cries, it gets annoying, and sometimes very annoying. I find my father's voice in the back of my head, when he used to get mad with us, where I think, *I've worked all day and I've worked so hard, and I come home and this is what I get?* And I'm horrified that I'm turning into my dad.

It is a relief to go to work sometimes. I think a lot of it is because at work I have a lot of autonomy. I have my own office. I actually have a lock on the door on my office, which was really nice when I was pumping at work. I remember when I put Cian in day care for the first time, I felt like Julie Andrews in the opening credits for *The Sound of Music*, where you're just spinning around and the birds are singing. There's times, even on the weekends, when I have to go in to work, it's a relief to go in and put on my music and just kind of sit there. And, you know, get something to eat. I don't have this little person wanting to eat it, too. Yeah, I think in a perfect world, I would work maybe twenty-five hours a week and then get the rest of those hours to myself. And then get Cian at, you know, maybe four in the afternoon and we'd have some time together. Then I would feel like I still have a life.

I'm just starting to get back into doing things that I like to do, mainly baking. And I just figure that I just have to plan a little bit more. I can't spontaneously decide on a Saturday morning, I'm gonna bake bread today. I need to have everything measured out like the night before. Even a couple weeks ago, on a weeknight I baked a cake. And I planned it out, and Cian just was not interested in cooperating, 'cause I was gonna put him to bed and bake the cake when he went down. And he just screamed and screamed and screamed. And I finally just baked the cake, listening to him screaming, and he finally fell asleep. I was wracked with guilt during it, because there is something, and maybe this is biological, there is something about your child crying. It just can induce the worst depression in me. You see where people can lose it, especially if they're tired.

I think a very positive thing about my working, as opposed to my maternity leave, is when we are together, I'm much more focused on him. Like today, we played with homemade play dough for at least an hour and a half and just had a really good time, and enjoyed reading our books and everything. When I was on maternity leave, I didn't really appreciate my time that much with him. I couldn't wait to have the me time. I love living in midtown, and I enjoy my job a lot, but sometimes I do feel like I have the golden handcuffs. Sometimes I feel I just wanna downsize and just go live in the country somewhere in a little house or have a simpler life. So I really don't know where we'll be.

Suzanne lives her new mantra

I have a new mantra now that's helped me a lot, and maybe that's why this is my new power outfit. It's "I'm doing the best I can. I'm doing the best I can."

Power is finally accepting myself for who I am. Power is being perfectly happy wearing these pants that I got at Old Navy when I was pregnant and was too fat to wear my pre-pregnancy pants and still being able to fit in them and they're not too big. And being okay with that. That's power to me now, and just sort of being okay with not going to the gym every day, being okay with the fact that my boobs sagged four inches, being okay that I have this huge varicose vein on my leg now, and slowly learning to be okay with knowing the fact that somewhere at any given point in time there's gonna be someone who's pissed off at me, and that's something I just have no control over. Being okay with chaos and being okay with being very imperfect. That's power.

France Garrido

Jersey City, New Jersey | August 2004

I'm a visual artist. I've been working in primarily collage and mixed media for twenty-five-plus years, and started doing this for Halloween and it sort of branched off. What I'm doing is creating another mask, which we all have, but this one becomes something that is obviously very creative. It evokes different things to the people that experience it and also for myself. If I go to an opening, it would be part of the fun of it, and just be in the vein of a happening, so to speak. Because it's a mask, it gives me permission to do things that I wouldn't normally do. I don't walk around like this all the time, so it allows me to experience people in another way as well.

I had this opening to go to, which I really wanted to go to. It was a beauti-

Trappings interview portrait,
Grace Church Van Vorst

ful exhibition with wonderful artists in it, and I just wasn't feeling myself. And I said, *Well, gee, if I cover myself, I won't be me anymore.* Of course I am, but, you know, maybe it'll just perk things up and I'll feel better about everything. So I did it, and it was the most amazing thing. As soon as I walked into the room, these three girls came up to me, they were probably eight years old, and they just flipped out. It wasn't really a performance, but it took on another whole aspect of this opening and they just took the ball and ran with it. I opened the cape and they went underneath it, and they started to play with it and they just were having such a wonderful time. That's part of the beauty as well. You can connect. I mean, there wasn't a person that came up to me that said, "What the fuck are you doing?" They all came up with a smile on their face. As soon as I walked in and those little girls came around me, I just forgot all that funk that I was in for the entire day. You realize at some point that it's daring, but it's me, it's still me. It's not this other person that comes out. You know, it's not a multiple personality disorder. To do something as zany as this, well, then I can walk into a corporation and say, "Blah blah blah, I need some money for art." It allows you to cross the boundaries in everyday life that you wouldn't normally do, and that's the real beauty of it.

I think to become or to act out that you're another person—movies do that for us, art does that for us, certainly—it all feeds into another world. When you talk about power, there's nothing that can really give you power except you, and that comes really from within. And however you get there, that's great, because as women, our power has been taken away for centuries, and we're struggling. Even though we've made some marks, it's still not equality. And power, personal power, financial power, are all things that we desire, and need, and want. One of my fears is that I lose my power. And then there's getting old. Getting old didn't bother me until I turned fifty, and then I realized that I wasn't twenty. I actually love being my age, and that gives us a sense of power. Yeah, I'm fifty. I don't have to ask permission to anyone, I don't have to do any of that anymore.

Well, my power comes from being able to make choices and being able to reach the goals that I want to reach for my life, and some of those goals have not materialized till now. And a lot of that has to do with spirituality and tapping into a place that is sacred and safe, but also it's a place where it's going into deep water. You go into the unconscious, and there's things that go on, and there's demons and there's light. Finding the light is where I want to be. I want to be in the light. I think that the exploration of my work is really an exploration of my life and my soul and my spirit, and that's what it's all about. There is nothing else to work on, there is nothing else to do. There's only that.

Susan Chin

Jersey City, New Jersey | November 2001

I'm an architect and I work at the Department of Cultural Affairs in New York City. I'm wearing my, let's see, dark suit with wide shoulders that I feel is my more powerful outfit. I guess, being in a field where men are predominant, that that is the way you need to express yourself. That you need to be conventional, like a man. Also wearing pants, you know, being on a scaffold, that they can't look up your skirt. That's not exactly the most powerful situation. And wearing earrings is important as distinguishing yourself from trying to be like a guy.

How do I feel that other people react to me when I'm in my outfit? I feel they regard me with authority. And isn't that what this is all about? It's about your inner expression of and confidence of who you are. You always stand out, and I think you're regarded with having more authority, or being smarter or brighter because you're there. Having the courage to be there. I think my approach with working with the construction workers was much more hands-on, being on the scaffold and telling them why we're building a wall in a certain way. I guess that you're regarded as being not the regular thing, but there's always a testing. They built a wall that

Trappings interview portrait,
Susan's office

needed to be ripped out, and I was like, "How can you guys do this? This is really embarrassing, and I know you could do better work than this." I think some other guy would have just yelled at them and said, "Rip it out!" Well, in my suit, you know, I could do that.

Well, it's an interesting dynamic, of being with men who are used to their wives or girlfriends being in a different role. And being a colleague. Right? Isn't that what it's all about? But you have to make that first impression. When you're meeting new people, I think it is very typical in New York that people judge you by your cover, and they don't know what your home life is like, they don't know what your family is all about, what your status is in society, and that's part of looking from the outside and then getting to know the inside. Which I think is sad, but it's what we are trained to look at.

And how to feel comfortable in your outfit, right? How to feel comfortable in what you're wearing, I think that is really an important part as well. Because if you're wearing really high heels and you're on a scaffold, I don't think that's exactly going to make you feel like you're in charge.

New York, New York | October 2006

When we first talked about clothing and power, we talked about having an image of yourself and how other people perceive you. I think that has deepened in me. Feeling like, *Is power perceived?* Is it how I'm perceiving you seeing me or is it how I feel about myself in a certain situation? I really have to say that power to me is not always in what you're wearing, it's your attitude about yourself and what you see as your position—what is it that you're powerful in or over?

I couldn't find something for you today that I was gonna pull out, put on, and say this is my power outfit. Right? This is my space suit. I really thought, *How do I talk about this today?* I've been at the Department of Cultural Affairs for eighteen years now. I've had influence in the work throughout the city and I know the process well enough, I feel secure enough that it's not about the clothes. Yes, I'd like to look nice. Everyone wants to be presentable, professional, and that's an expectation.

For me a really important thing is intellect and intellectual stimulation. My Loeb Fellowship to Harvard at the Graduate School of Design was a really pivotal moment in taking the episodic work that I do of creating capital projects, creating new wings at museums, or various exhibits, or theaters, and connecting them in the neighborhood or connecting them in the city. How do we create those networks of both the cultural community as well as the public?

Susan at home

Last year, I was president of the American Institute of Architects' New York Chapter. First Asian woman, first public sector architect to serve in this capacity. We're about to celebrate the 150th anniversary of the New York Chapter. This is a very significant year for us. I'm not the first woman; there have been maybe five or six women in the 150 years.

I don't think of being an authority. I think of myself as just being a participant at the table. So maybe, you know, extensions of your clothing as extensions of yourself? Thinking of other ways of extending yourself. Is it through the work? Is it through your staff and the intellect of other people? Is it everybody contributing to making our society better? That sounds so hokey and idealistic, but I think that we do want it to be a better place.

Talking about clothes as a façade, do you have a façade around yourself? Do you build a wall around yourself? Or is it a protective layer? Or is it that you are dressing for the role? Or you're role-playing? How to feel comfortable enough to say, *I'll let you in, you can see who I really am, the whole person*? That's something that I've never been that comfortable with. Is it my Asian-ness? Maybe that's part of it. You don't show everybody everything. This is really getting into something that is related to who I really am. As an Asian person, you are brought up to be very private about your life. I love being around people—do they really always know who I am? This is like full circle: Is it who you perceive who I am? And how do I express to you my role, my authority, my influence?

I'm already wearing my outfit. I have an Asian face. I'm third-generation Chinese American, but people have their own perception already about who I am by just looking at me, and maybe this is where clothes, a certain outfit makes the difference. I'm not wearing a Mao suit or whatever, but how to be comfortable with that as well. If you just think I'm just off the boat, so be it. I kind of write you off.

Jan Gallaway

Pittsburgh, Pennsylvania | June 2004

I'm a member of the Pittsburgh Puffins. I'm forty-seven. I started when I was forty-three. The reason I picked my hockey gear was because I examined what power was in my life. I have always been an athlete, and as early as I can remember I've been in some part of a team. I came into ice hockey because when I was younger I was a figure skater and the skills are transferable. And it is just a blast.

Pittsburgh Puffins practice and Jan's interview session

Trappings interview portrait,
Mary L. Pretz-Lawson's home

I want to talk about what it is like to put on the gear, because it is very different for a woman to put on shoulder pads. We actually wear a cup. We wear knee pads, elbow pads. And the first time I put it on, it was like, *Wow, this is what it feels like.* I felt like, *This is so cool, I can actually run into a wall or run into a person and not injure myself or injure them either.* Well, you know, sort of. We do wear mouth guards and a full face shield. Everybody has to have teeth on Monday morning, that's what I always say.

A lot of our skaters started skating within the last five years. Once you get it into your blood, you kind of get hooked on it. At least we did. You would be surprised, like in Pittsburgh there's probably eight skating rinks, and about nine, ten o'clock at night if you stand at any of the rinks there are tons and tons of adult men players. It's a large sport in this city. I don't like to play with men, they're too rough. They don't like it when you beat 'em. When you beat them to a puck or skate faster, then they are vindictive. Then they want to hurt you. So I prefer to play all women rather than co-ed. Being on a team is really fun, and interesting to know the women. You rely on them in different ways, different strengths and weaknesses. That component of being in a group is something I like and will probably seek out if I can't skate competitively anymore.

When you skate, you glide, your hair is going, and you actually can pummel people. Most of our players are forty and above. The first year that we started to play, every time someone would fall, we'd be helping them up. We have progressed to the point where we are very aggressive and assertive and we want to score and win. It's fun to be strong. It's fun to be physically strong and to know you are looking at a twenty-year-old—and honey, look out. You can't substitute youth for power at our age.

One time I was walking in the hallway. It was so funny. There were these little boys and they saw us. They were like, "Oh my God, they're our mothers!" You know what, they don't know until the end of the game when you shake hands and take your helmet off. You hear gasps, audible gasps.

Sure, anyone could want to be a team player, but an even playing field is made for girls when they are given access to sports funding without having to petition for resources before they begin. Title IX is the 1972 law that requires educational institutions to maintain policies, practices, and programs that do not discriminate against anyone based on sex. Beyond making it possible for girls to play on teams, the law prohibits sexual harassment of anyone in the educational environment (both students and teachers) and forbids schools from discriminating against girls who become pregnant.

Pat Clements Jaquay

New York, New York | February 2004

I'm a native New Yorker, born in Brooklyn, raised in Long Island for the most part. I'm a single mother of two grown children, almost twenty-five and almost twenty-three. I've been a career sales professional for thirty years. I worked for IBM for eighteen years, I worked for Cisco, Xerox, Kodak, and most recently became a stockbroker and worked for UBS Financial Services. And I currently am in my own business. I'm a business development consultant. I decided to go out on my own about three months ago.

As far as what makes me feel powerful, I was one of the first women hired at IBM into sales, predominantly a male organization. At that time, similar to a lot of the banks, IBM had a very strict dress code. The men wore blue suits and white shirts and a striped tie, and the women all wore skirted suits or dresses. We were not allowed to wear slacks of any sort or a pantsuit. So my first day of work, 1974, I showed up with a whole new wardrobe. I had hair down to here and I came to work with short hair like this and the boss said, "Who's that, where's that girl I hired?" I said, "Well, she's gone. The woman is here."

It was all men—just Margo Johnson and myself. The clients needed education because they didn't know how to deal with women. Lots of the things that went on in those days could have people arrested right now. But you dealt with it. On one occasion I went back to the office after I was mistreated by a client and I told my boss. He was a big, big, Irish guy, and he said, "Get your coat." We went back there, and he told this guy that if he ever did anything like that to any of his people again he'd be in jail. So that was reinforcement that at least I had somebody at IBM that was going to back me up, that believed me. Because in those days if a woman was harassed, or raped even, it was usually the woman's fault.

It's interesting, I think I traded one kind of uniform for this kind of a uniform, the business uniform. I went to Catholic school, so I wore a uniform and gloves and a hat every day for twelve years to school. Coming into a corporate environment such as IBM was really very comfortable because I came from a very strict Irish-Catholic background. My father worked for a bank for forty-five years, and he wore the blue suit and the white shirt and the striped tie every day to work. My mother was a homemaker, very strict, very classical environment as far as roles and so forth. And I was the only girl in the family, so there weren't a lot of options for me. I tried college for about a semester. The Vietnam War was on, all my friends were overseas fighting a war, and all the long-haired hippie freaks were smokin' dope and picketing on the cam-

puses. And I said, *I can't do this. I have to go to work because it's making me angry to go to school every day and watch these people that don't want to go and defend our country be dissidents.* All the people that were important to me were overseas. I was writing letters every week to all these boys. I wanted to go into the service myself, but my brother was an officer in the army, and he told me he would break both my legs if I went in. I decided that wasn't a good option, so I went to work.

I started working in New York City at nineteen. I was also working volunteer work at the hospital on the weekends, and I was going to school at night. So I had a lot of stuff going on. I'm a master at the juggling act. My greatest accomplishment is that I was able to have a life for myself. One of the things that helps me to feel more in control is that I work on my spiritual life. I work on being independent. I work on the fact that I don't need anybody else to help me pay my bills. I don't need anybody else to help me make a decision. I have my own home. I've raised my children. It reinforces the fact that I have control over my life and over my decisions every day. And the way I walk down the street sends a message, too, because

Trappings interview portrait, conference room, Baruch College

I'm very in tune with control because my father was very much in control. And I have brothers, who, you know, they walked on water and the girl was kind of like, you know, a second-class citizen to some degree. We've come a long way.

I still am pretty much the same person that I was growing up. I still am a dancer. I've been on television a couple of times, just casual stuff where cameras show up. I happen to be a very good dancer, so I usually get on camera. And I also sing. I sing and dance on the outside, but I was able to bring a lot of my creative, uh, function to the business world.

And some of my best awards, at IBM in particular, were when I was really bored. I'd sit up at 590 Madison and I'd look out the window and I'd think, *Now, what am I gonna do to liven myself up here and make my work life more interesting?* I would put these huge deals together and then I'd get an award for it. And we'd get more business out of it because it was really something that was meaningful to the client.

Speaking of clients, when I present to a client, I always wear a suit. I always wear a skirted suit. With rare exception—if it's really zero temperature, I might wear a pantsuit. But if I'm closing a deal, I want to make sure that the client knows that I mean business when I show up, and I also don't want to look like the boys. I like to show my legs because it's one of my best assets, but as you can see by my skirt, it's not too provocative. The message is that when I show up in a suit, I took the time to dress to that client, and he or she knows that I'm there to do business, I'm not there for a social call.

So I think that your dress really communicates what your message is. I always say to my kids, "You never have a second chance to make a good first impression." I stand by that because my mom, when I was a kid, she used to put her lipstick on and comb her hair to go walk the dog. And she'd always say, "You never know who you're going to run into." And that's pretty much the way I live my life. Every day I want to be ready. If I meet the Pope or I meet the President or my Next Love, I want to be ready. I want to have my lipstick on and my hair combed.

I have capabilities and I'm able to function just as well as a man can. And I don't have to dress like a man, I don't have to act like a man, but I do business like a business person. Take the sex part of it out. And I think it's taken a whole generation of women like me fighting the battles and pushing back. I said it to my daughter, who's almost twenty-three, "You have no idea how much easier it is for you." All these young girls are so much more fortunate because the trailblazers, the baby boomers, my generation, we had to fight the battles and, you know, kind of shut up or put up. Women were not supposed to speak up for themselves. Women were not supposed to show that they were smart or capable or independent, but now it's different. The sky's the limit, which is great for them. I feel like I'm a part of it, so it's my reward.

Floral Park, New York | October 2006

The time that we last met, I was embarking on a new business for myself. 2004 was probably the toughest year I've ever had, other than the year I left my husband—with two babies on a bus. I knew it took three years to kind of break even.

I just worked. Worked and worked and worked and worked and slept and ate and went back to work again. The second year it got a little bit easier, and the money, the pipeline, started to fill. This is my third year, and I see a significant difference from a financial perspective from last year to this, and next year is going to be a real increase. So all the work and sacrifice and doing without social events because I didn't have the money, I didn't have the time, and I was too tired in most cases to carry on a conversation, it worked out. Now I'm in a position that I'm on my own. Nobody dictates how I spend my days.

I have a lot more flexibility now in my life. And my children have left, which is a real significant change in my financial picture, too, because I don't have to split my check in three ways anymore. Hallelujah. My son left in January of 2004, and my daughter left in December of that year, and my dog of thirteen years was gone. And my mother went into a nursing home that year. I always thought being a good mother was the most important thing that I could have done, ever. So that was a real sense of loss and a very big change in my status, and feelings of my self-worth, because all of a sudden a big piece of me, the mommy piece, was gone. I think that one of the best things you can do for your children is to push them out of the nest and make them grow up, because eventually, they have to grow up anyway, so they're better off making the mistakes early rather than late. It's really paid off. Both of my children have acknowledged that I did the right thing.

I think as you get older, your experiences in life reinforce you, and what doesn't kill you will make you stronger. I thought about this so often. You know, some of the best growth in my life has been when I was just about on my knees, exhausted, trying to raise kids, trying to do it all, trying to pay the bills, and trying to be a performer at work. There were times when I just felt like I just wanted to sit down and cry, but couldn't. Who cared?

Power has changed for me. Now I think that is confidence and peace of mind. I've gone through the struggle of raising the children. I've gone through the struggle of being a high performer. I think having gone through the transition that I've just made over the last couple of years has proven to me that, you know, I don't have to be the IBM person, I don't have that label on. 'Cause that was powerful in itself. I would walk in and I'd say, "I'm from IBM" or "I'm from Cisco" or "I'm from Xerox." People would say, "Oh, come right in." Now I'm on my own. The power comes in knowing yourself and being at peace in who you are and not having to really impress anybody.

I could never go back to the corporate culture. When I was younger, it was a very nurturing environment, but because of changes in the economy and all the downsizing that's going on, people are really required to do so much more work than they were ten, fifteen years ago. There's so much pressure for the numbers, and the bottom line, and the performance, that I really think that Corporate America has missed the boat on creativity and productivity. Because people are stressed, and they're tired, and they're worn down, you don't get the best from them. And people are worried, looking over their shoulders, worrying whether I'm going to go or is it Joe next to me? So I think that there's no such thing as going back to what corporate life was like twenty, thirty years ago. It just doesn't exist anymore.

At Pat's home

The diamond, you know, it is created under tremendous pressure, and when it's taken out of the ground it's black and pretty ugly. When it's cleaned up and cut, it's one of the most beautiful gems. I use that analogy for life itself because I am living proof that the harder it is the better you get. I always get what I want, but it doesn't always come in my time. Most of them aren't really materialistic things, they're things that are more performance related, personal development related. The only things that I've ever bought for myself were a house, and a car, and a fortieth birthday present. Which I couldn't afford then, but I put one hundred dollars down and kept going back and paying a little bit. I had the guy take a picture of me with my ring on, and I put it on my refrigerator, and I said, "I'm going to get that ring." And I did.

Megan Jones

Memphis, Tennessee | October 2002

I became a business owner about a year and a half ago. The transformation and how I felt about powerful, and being powerful, and needing power, and acting like I had power, all came together in a very jarring way for me. One of the unexpected consequences that I encountered is that the more I have felt discriminated against, or run into sexual stereotypes, the sexier my clothes have become. Just to let you know, this is what I wore to work today.

Trappings interview portrait,
Carissa Hussong's home

My clothing has become a rebellious, inappropriate way of confronting the problems that I have come across. A lot of that has been multi-tiered. That a smart woman can't be sexy, that a sexy woman can't be smart. That sex is powerful, but only in a realm that doesn't intersect with business. I have really enjoyed the times it has made people uncomfortable in a vicious, petty manner. I have enjoyed the sense of upset that I think it gets me sometimes within meetings, to have people put off balance by the fact that they see a slice of tummy, or my shirt is a little bit too low, or the skirt is a little bit too tight, or the boots are a little on the dominatrix side. And so even though sometimes I've regretted it later, I've done things like worn an all-leather suit to a presentation to an investment boutique in Little Rock, Arkansas, which is not known for its, um, liberal attitudes.

The leather suit was very calculated. I knew that everybody else, male and female, was going to be wearing a suit. There was only one other female in the meeting. She was very subordinate to me, in terms of position. I was very cognizant of wanting to project a different kind of image that would force a different perspective on them. Meaning, *Hey, you haven't paid attention to this kind of thing in a long time, this is something necessary for you to compete. I want you to look at me and talk to me before, during, and after the meeting.*

I actually had a pretty upsetting moment when I walked in. I was carrying my laptop, the projector, a box full of leave-behinds. I'm waddling in with all this shit, and I'm dumping it down in the conference room, and one of the other vendors who was presenting, one of the guys, who's a complete jerk, looked at me and said, "Did you get that suit where Dennis Rodman shops?" I just remember looking at

The leather suit that rocked Little Rock

him and I said, "That is the most unpleasant comment. And inappropriate to start this meeting." And he was very taken aback. And for about the next thirty minutes, while their part of the meeting went on, I was very self-conscious. But by the time I got up, I was just kind of like, *Fuck it, this is what I chose to wear. There's nothing wrong with it. I bought it at Banana Republic, they're not in the business of selling whips-and-chains suits. And I look very nice.*

So the clothing has always kind of been there, and I think what's happened is that I've been more cognizant about how I use it to manipulate the situation. If you're caught wearing your Ms. Kitty's Pussycat Lounge tank top, you know, unawares, you're not in a powerful situation. If you engineer the encounter so you're the one surprising the board meeting in your leather suit, then, you know, it's all good to go. So it's been a real eye-opener to me in that way.

I think that the necessary ingredients for me, for power, are boots, definitely a must. If boots can't be worn because it's summertime, then it's high heels. Tall is always good. Boots are easier 'cause you don't have to shave your legs. Any kind of element of surprise or whimsy or sex that's thrown into the mix I think is very important. And a lot of confidence, an incredible amount. I think the clothes that I've chosen have definitely evolved down that line. I'm a woman, I'm making money. I may be taking your money, and you know, I'm in your face about it. And I think that's been, for good or bad, the kind of path that I've wandered down. I'm very interested to see what happens in the next two years, if I do need to rely on the clothing to retain that powerful feeling or if I can move past it to say, *Yeah, I feel powerful today* in something that is either more conservative or revealing. And I have to say at this point in time I can't foresee that happening.

I was watching the Mary Kay story last night with Shirley MacLaine, and she was telling the television interviewer that when she looks good she finds that both men and women treat her better. And I don't know if that's sad but true or just true and true. I think it's just true and true, actually. It's been a really big form of entertainment, for definitely the women. I have had a couple of comments this year from male colleagues that I'm friends with: "Hey, Megan, did you know that your clothes are getting sexier this year? I mean, what's going on? You used to be so conservative." And I don't choose to answer that for them. The reasons for doing it are none of their business. If they enjoy it, that's great, and if they're uncomfortable, that's great, too. That's just an added bonus for me.

Memphis, Tennessee | March 2006

Since 2002, I have been really lucky in terms of business. We've added new partners, new clients. It has been an interesting journey. Although I've been very satisfied with it at times, I also find it to be the loneliest job I've ever had. Being a small business owner is hard. It's a very difficult, intense endeavor, and if anyone ever told you what was involved with a small business, no one would ever do it. On the other end of the stick, I feel like everybody should own a small business at least once in their lives, so that they fully understand what it's like to be responsible for your own destiny and for the lives of others. So that's been incredible.

I started a book about aggressive dressing, which I think is a little bit different than power dressing. This is dressing to intimidate, to get what you want. It's feminism but in a different vein. I conceived of the idea of kind of making this book like a military manual, so I called it *The F-100*. It took situations and then gave you ideas for appropriate dress for each, based upon the premise that you're trying to gain an edge over the situation, an opponent, or simply another person. What to wear to an interview, a presentation, a first date, a second date, a third date, that kind of thing. At the end of it, I had a list of basically like weapons of mass destruction for fashion—it was things like turtlenecks, baseball caps, any shoes that you can hear, that flop: bad. I can list them forever.

Here're the things that connote power. An open neckline, not being afraid to expose your throat because you are so powerful and it doesn't matter. For a lot of women, that really elongates them. To have pieces that are unfinished, and undone, and odd, I think that's what gives you confidence. I think that's what makes dressing a pleasure instead of, you know, *How am I gonna dress today to hide the fact that I have ten extra pounds?* Well, that sucks, that sucks for anybody, you know?

One of the things that has distressed me is that I feel that women more and more are being used as advertisements. This huge push, or fad, or trend, or cycle that we're going through where there's an extreme makeover. Like, you were okay before, but now that you have the right jeans and you've put on some mascara, you look so much better and your life is gonna be changed. There's numerous television shows packaged for the female contingent that are all about bringing women up to an acceptable level of consumption. Right? About making you conform to this certain level of beauty, whereas I was thinking that clothing is expression. It's not about making sure that someone knows that you have a Gucci bag.

I'm not a billboard. I don't wanna be a billboard. When I was a kid, my mom never bought me Izods or Gloria Vanderbilt jeans, or any of the things that I wanted. It used to piss me off. I couldn't understand it. And her point was if you're gonna wear somebody else's logo, they need to pay you. You don't need to pay them. And that really resonated with me. We were not allowed to watch *Charlie's Angels*, we were not allowed to watch beauty pageants, we were not allowed to wear clothing with status items or icons on it. I think at the time that was all just crappy, but looking back on it, boy, that informed a

The Yes Dress

lot of who I am, how I look at other women, and how I look at myself, how I judge, and the value I place on the things that I buy. So, very seminal.

My clothes are a tool. So, for instance, this dress, It's called my Yes Dress because when I am asking someone for something and I want good results, I wear the Yes Dress. It's this really interesting combination of a strong color, the reds, so I get to wear red shoes, but it's also nude. It's like being nude with a tattoo. Every morning I get up and I look at my calendar and I see what I've got to do, and that's how I pick my clothing. It's like, who do I have to talk to, what do I have to accomplish, what do I have to wear to accomplish that?

It's a shame that there aren't more self-proclaimed fashionable feminists out there. I think people, not just women, let other people define what that means to them. Right? They think that it means Gloria Steinem. They think it means bra burning and women with really short haircuts and no sense of humor who are all holding up signs for abortion rights. And, you know, to me, what it means is being able to be an equitable, respected part of society. It means being able to command the same amount of pay for the same work, big time. It means trying to fit in a family with having an economic impact in your life and in other people's lives. That's something that I think has been diffi-cult as a small business owner to do.

But I think power to me is being able to persuade, cajole, or force other people to do things that they normally would not do. And I also think that is power enacted upon others. Feeling powerful within yourself, I think, proba-bly my definition of that is a little bit more liquid, it's not as rigid. Maybe four years ago, or even maybe two years ago, I would have said it means being inde-pendent, it means being able to support yourself, and it means being able to do whatever the hell you wanna do. But now, I think sometimes powerful peo-ple are the ones who can be soft, and I haven't necessarily learned that.

Georgia Boley

This is the outfit that I wore when I graduated at the University of Wyoming, my undergraduate degree. I don't think I ever picked this outfit out thinking about power, and I don't think I've ever picked clothes out with that word in my head, but maybe I was subconsciously hoping that these clothes displayed power. I think the reason I picked this outfit, eight years ago, was because I was wooing my man, who happens to be my husband now. I was looking for something very sexy and tight and, you know, showing my curves as much as I could, and not necessarily comfort. I had different shoes on, white sexy sandals, which I don't even own anymore. I didn't try it on until a couple of hours ago. I was so proud of myself, I couldn't believe I could even get into this.

The other outfit that I have probably is the strongest theme in my life as far as what makes me feel a sense of who I am. I am from the West. I was born and raised in the West and I'm very much a cowgirl, and I've worked on ranches, I've wrangled on ranches. I have a cowboy hat that's floated down the Shoshone River, my horse and me tumbled through the river. I should've worn that. It's probably the strongest theme in my life, and I have

Trappings interview portrait,
Tami Davis's home

a feeling will be the theme that will stay in my life through all the other themes that come and go. So that's a very powerful outfit. And maybe what comes with that: living in the West, the boots, the belt, the hat. It's manly as well, it's somewhat unisex. I've done some very powerful things in that outfit, that cowboy outfit.

When I was a little girl, I would have boy days where I'd wear jeans and say, "I'm not sitting with my sister or my mom, I'm sitting with my dad because I'm a boy today." I'd go to school and I'd say, "I'm a boy," just to try it on and see what people would say. And my parents didn't make a big deal of it, so I realized it was kind of boring to do, and I moved on. But I've always envied women that had a sense of womanly and were able to really feel sexy and know it. Because you can sense when a woman in a room knows that they have that power.

I think the strongest thing for me, when I hear the words *power* and *women*, is to not be afraid of the womanly view of being powerful because so much of my life, power is looking like a man. And the cowgirl outfit is very much more manly than what I'm wearing tonight. So I think that this is the right outfit. That maybe it's a little more controversial in my mind for myself, about power, but I think it's right. Being a woman is very powerful. It doesn't have to be anything like a man.

Sheridan, Wyoming | April 2004

It was interesting how when you really find out exactly who you are, and what makes you *you,* is when you go somewhere else where you're not in your element. And that was when I went to graduate school at Case Western Reserve in Cleveland, Ohio. The girls that were in my internship with me, the interests they had were so not what I was interested in at all. Fishing, hunting, horses, they had absolutely no interest in any of that. You know, they shopped. They knew what Gap was selling and The Limited was selling, and I was excited to know what Limited and Gap were, but certainly wasn't thinking about it on the weekends, or, you know, when I wasn't studying. There's two malls in this state, and there's like a mall every five miles in Cleveland.

I'm very much academically oriented. But then I got kids, and it makes the balance of when am I a dietitian, when am I a mom, when am I wife, and all the things I want to be, hard to find. It's really hard to find because I want to be all of them, but I also want to be really good at all of them. So some of them have to wait. The dietitian part is just a nine-to-five job right now.

It's harder and harder to live a western life. Even in Wyoming, you can't really make a living being a cowboy. It's not a living. It's a way of life. You have to have a way to make money. And so my husband, who is definitely a cowboy, ropes competitively, but he has no time, he works fifty-plus hours a week at his white-collar job.

These are tight-fitting jeans, and these are elk-hide boots. They're pretty tough, that's why I picked them out. This belt means a lot to me. Belts are a significant part of a cowgirl or -boy outfit, very significant part. This was my grandmother's belt from Mexico. It's real gold. My grandma epitomizes what Wyoming is to me. She was always working with her hands and outside. Very much the ranch hand's wife, or the ranchwoman.

Georgia on her ranch

I should tell you, this hat has a lot of significance. I was a wrangler on this dude ranch outside of Yellowstone. I brought my own horse, which very few people do, but I figured this horse was three, and he really needed to be ridden. I thought, *How great, I can get paid to ride my own horse.* They very nicely let me do that.

There was this Shoshone River there, and it was during spring runoff when people do rapids down it. It's a very large river, large for Wyoming stan-

dards. My boss had told us to never, never go against whatever he said on the trail or else we would be immediately fired. He was kind of a jerk. And well, he wants to cross the river, and he's crazy. I was the only one that was from Wyoming, and I felt like the only one who really understood what spring runoff was. You don't cross the river in June just because you can cross it in August. It's totally different. But I didn't want to lose my job, and this horse that I was on has been across rivers and swam quite a bit, so we went across it. I think my horse saved my life, because he went underneath the water and I could see him doing circles in front of me. I think he broke the current, so that I didn't crash into rocks. He crashed into some rocks and went to a place where there was no way we could reclaim him. There was another wrangler that went down and cut my saddle off of him for me, but he was dead. This hat was on me through the whole thing. Well, I thought at the time it was like losing a child, now I know it's nothing like that. A lot of other riders lost their horses, but nobody else died. Thank God. I mean, we had eight-year-olds on this ride.

Yeah, a John Wayne wannabe. My first response was just total anger. I was pissed. The first thing I said is, "You owe me a horse." My first response always is anger to things like that. A lot of women respond like emotionally and cry. I don't know what it is about me. I just get mad. He did pay for the value of the horse, and I finished working there that summer. I didn't quit.

Courtney Wilson

Pittsburgh, Pennsylvania | June 2004

The reason why I feel this outfit is powerful is because I think it reflects my personality the best. I'm a very outgoing person, I like to be flamboyant. I like people to look at me, and that itself is powerful.

I know that men will look at me in this outfit and they'll whisper to their friends. Women will look at me in this outfit and whisper to their friends, "Oh you bitch." Or whatever. If you're having people talking about you, that's power. You're impacting their lives for maybe a minute, two minutes— even if they're saying something negative, it's still powerful.

I am into laboratory research, which means I spend the day in the lab all day long. At work, you don't dress at all because you're not judged on power by what you're wearing, you're judged on power by your mental ability. So I wear the crappiest clothes I have to work. They get dirty because I'm working with dangerous chemicals, radioactivity and things like that, so I don't want to get anything on good clothes. There, power is judged completely upon your skills and your intelligence.

Most of those people don't really do the things that I do. I don't usually go out to a club or something before mid-

Trappings interview portrait,
Tara McComb's home

night, so those people are mainly in bed. If I was seen in these clothes at my job, I think people would have a lesser opinion of my intelligence, just because I'm exuding my sexuality instead of being inward and exuding my intelligence.

Courtney in her work clothes

I think that women should be allowed to dress however they want. I won't pass judgment on someone that is dressed more conservative. It's just their personality. But if I see someone that's dressed like me, that's awesome. I think it's great and I'd probably be more apt to talk to them and try to make friends with them because I think they'd be more like me.

I believe I am a very sexual person and I also believe I am a very intelligent person. To balance those out is kinda difficult. That's why I kinda keep them separate. It's easier for me to let loose in a social situation than it is at work. When I'm in a social situation I don't like people to know that I am a laboratory researcher, because then the whole focus of the conversation goes to the job, and I go out to get away from the job. If I push it to the limit on both situations, then I have both sides of myself satisfied, so I don't feel the need to intermingle them. But having them both satisfied makes me comfortable and makes me assured of myself.

I used to not dress this way. I used to dress very androgynous with very baggy clothes all the time. I had a boyish haircut, things like that. And once I came to grips with the fact that I'm a woman, then I decided to start exuding my sex-

Courtney getting ready for a night out

uality and not hiding it. I think that that started probably about four or five years ago. And I've come to be very comfortable showing my body. It actually feels pretty good to not be under wraps, so to speak. I think some of it has to do with compliments from other people. Some of it has to do with becoming a woman, some of it just has to do with being crazy, I guess, and just letting it all hang out. I'm prepped to go out and shock the world and amaze the men and have the women call me a bitch and everything.

Anna B. Sandoval Girón

Wellesley Hills, Massachusetts | October 2005

I was born in Guatemala. And I just moved to Boston in August. I am a professor at Simmons College in the department of sociology. Power comes from being comfortable. And it's been a long struggle to find stuff that I like how it looks and it's also comfortable. So even the suits I own are really, really comfortable.

And the t-shirt, I saw it in San Diego. I was going through this weird stage, like having issues with men, and I thought, *That would be so cool to wear for a date.* So I bought it. I also bought one that says FUCK FASHION. I thought, *This is so cool,* and then I started wearing it and I realized this is so fun to wear because particularly men get offended. It's like, Oh, are you really that good? And I haven't been able to wear it because I can't show up and teach in a t-shirt that says I'M TOO GOOD FOR YOU, nor in one that says FUCK FASHION. So, you know, I've been missing the outfits.

I went on this date with this guy. Actually, maybe I was wearing this same outfit. He was really into himself—really cute, really charming young man, but way full of himself. And I wanted a black t-shirt, so I put this on, and when I arrived, he was really offended. He was like, "I can't walk down the street with you, wearing that. What is that gonna say about me?" And I'm like, "It's not saying anything about you. It just goes well with my outfit." And there was this whole conversation about, Do you really mean it? I realized, Yeah, I kind of really mean it.

Then I realized, like, people do react to it. I went shopping with this shirt and this woman was like, "Oh my God, you're so brave. I always wanted to own a shirt that says that." And it's great to go in a bar by myself. Like, honestly, a great thing. It's like, *Don't get near me. I'm here for a drink, not to pick up a guy.*

I think power means having control over my decisions. It's almost like I can control my life in a way that I have never been able to do before. Like now, I finally feel that I have full control. My life is not in the control of an adviser, or a committee, or funding for graduate school. Now it's about me making the decisions I want to make. That's really what power is. Also, being able to choose what I wanna wear, what I wanna say, where I wanna be.

I do Latin American studies. But I'm really interested in doing work in Central America, because it's like a forgotten land. Nobody really cares about Central America, and we're told we're Mexican, which we're not, with all due respect to Mexican people. Central Americans have their own identity.

My work is very personal, and it's also political. What I do work on is looking at what happened after the signing of the peace treaties in Guatemala, how civil society kind of fell apart, and all the violence that emerged from that, kidnappings for ransom, murders, and all of that. And I became interested in that when friends got murdered and friends got kidnapped. A lot of

us were being shipped out of the country, and that's one of the reasons why I came to the U.S., too. We were all shipped in this massive exodus. Parents who could afford sent us out.

I decided to go back and kind of study what happened to our whole generation of kids that had to leave. And the whole idea—if we understand it, we can fix it. Because I don't think that we have a really clear understanding of what's going on. So that's kind of what I do.

The decision to come to college in the U.S. completely shifted my world and my life. Now that I'm saying that, I think the other big one is when I did my field research. My mom died of breast cancer and I decided to go home to spend two years with her, and now I'm gonna cry . . .

Going home was, like, the best decision. I think it made me realize that academia was not the only thing in the world, which is really good because that's what you're trained to

Trappings interview portrait,
Jill Taylor's home

think in graduate school. And it made me realize that I really did want to have a life in which I could spend time with my family and be around them. I managed to get this relationship as grown-ups with my siblings, which had never happened before. It was a hard decision because I had to leave behind a whole life and a relationship that I was involved in, but it was also really good because I realized, *Wow, my family's actually kind of a cool bunch.* They're quite nice people, and I hadn't ever really acknowledged that as an adult. I realized I'm very privileged to have that, because a lot of people just don't like their family. I always think about that. I kind of miss them, not in a weird way, but I miss them and their presence in my life. So it was a really, really good decision to go there and then come back.

Rachelle Nesta

Laramie, Wyoming | March 2005

I'm a senior in women's studies and sociology here at the University of Wyoming. I wore this dress because I have deemed myself Feminist Barbie because I am a Barbie. In kindergarten, I wore a dress every day to school except two. One day must have just been a fluke on my part, but the other day I had on a dress and I slipped and fell in the mud. My mom had to bring me clothes. She brought me sweatpants. I was really devastated because it was like, *Mom, I've worn a dress every day, I'm in a dress today, and you bring me sweatpants?* Like how much more mortifying could it get? Then I was changing—she forgot my panties, too. So I thought everyone would know I didn't have on underwear, but it all turned out fine. I'm a feminist who would love to go to a ball every day.

One of my friends, who's an artist, made a feminist Barbie. She took it out of the box and changed the box, and the Barbie had on like pants and was real earthy and all these things. I thought, *You know what? That's not me.* I'm the Barbie in the box that just has on this huge dress and like prom hair. And I thought, *You know what, like, Feminist Barbie exists. I am her.* Generally, you think of Barbie and you think, Oh, that's bad. You know, she has this body that nobody can ever achieve, who really

Trappings interview portrait,
Student Center, University of Wyoming

takes her seriously? But I think that I know who I am. I'm so feminine. I mean, I collect Barbies. I wear pink. I'm very active in the feminist community. I love women's studies, I'm gonna go to school and get a PhD so I can teach it someday. I would love to start a women's studies program at a university that doesn't have one, or become the director of it. I am so passionate about women's studies and feminism, but at the same time I'm this very stereotypical female that loves to dress up and loves to look her best. I think it throws people.

My mother is very strong and so are my grandmothers. So I've always had this in me. I've always been one for reproductive rights, but then I came to college, and my cousin had taken a women's studies course. And she said, "Oh, you should take this. You'd love it." So I took intro to women's studies, and I would just not shut up in that class. I found out about the feminist group here on campus and got to know some of the girls in that. I guess it's all history from there.

My mom is a feminist who does not identify as one 'cause I think she doesn't really understand that she is one. After taking my women's studies course, I would kind of dialogue with my mom about what I'm learning. Every time I go home, for the first couple of semesters I'd always hit them with something new, and they'd say, "Oh, how's this?" And I'll be like, "That's just wrong. Don't you understand how patriarchal that is?" She'll say something, and I will disagree, or agree, or bring up a different point. She's just like, "Okay, I see it from your point of view." She doesn't lose her opinion necessarily, but she does always see my point. I still don't think my family totally understands my activism.

I remember we were driving down the street and it was in February and they had up a big thing about Martin Luther King. And she goes, "Do you do that, too?" And I was like, "What does that mean, do I do that, too?" And she's like, "You know, fighting. Whatever you do." I was like, "Okay, that's not my issue, but yes I do support that, and yes I would go to marches like that and everything."

Last night we were at this fun party for a new group that's being started on campus, Voices for Planned Parenthood. Women's Action Network, the feminist group on campus, was approached by Planned Parenthood to start this group to advocate for reproductive rights and to educate the women in Wyoming about the services that are available to them, even if they're not necessarily in their city. There's a Planned Parenthood in Casper, and that's the only Planned Parenthood in Wyoming. We have an abortion clinic in Jackson.

Right now, I'm working on my internship putting together a conference for all the state leaders who are concerned with women's issues. There was a report that just came out, they graded them on women's health and reproductive rights, and Wyoming scored D minus because we do only have that one clinic and it's not real accessible.

People tend to sometimes think, like, Oh, there's this blond, blue-eyed, short girl. And I think that sometimes I get taken for granted, or people don't look past that. But at the same time, this is probably bad to say, but sometimes I use that to my advantage. Like, if you know that there's a male who's in charge of some program, and you need something for a discount, well, I will wear a low-cut shirt, because guess what? I get the discount. And that's really unfortunate. Like I hate that I do that, but when I'm gonna go somewhere and present myself in a professional manner, I might make sure that I look a little more feminine or kind of fit that stereotypical role just a little bit more, because sometimes it does get me places. But I hate that it does. I really do. I hate that it does.

Uruj Sheikh

I graduated from the Academy of St. Aloysius, and I'm gonna be a freshman at Pace University in New York City. I think that power is like the energy that you give off. I think everyone has something unique about them, maybe it's their sense of humor, or maybe they enjoy drawing or taking pictures or writing. I think that once you submerge yourself into what you enjoy, I think that's power.

I really—I really enjoy fashion. I love buying clothes and going shopping, but I think that people should wear things that make them feel comfortable. Clothes help you give off a certain energy, like a very confident energy. That's why I say sometimes I use clothes to help me feel more confident about myself, 'cause, you know, when you look good you feel good.

I love traditional Pakistani clothing. We have, like, a lot of beading and sequins on our clothing. They're very showy and I like that about our clothing. It gives off our personality. We have to have long shirts, you know, for modesty, but the men and the women do it. But sometimes, like in Pakistan or any other Muslim countries, they wear regular American clothing, too. Because, you know, a lot of those countries are becoming Westernized.

It feels really good when other people from other cultures see you in your clothes. It's like inviting them into your culture. Like letting them see who you really are. Because like in America, we all kind of dress alike, we all wear American clothing. But when people wear clothing from other countries, it's like an invitation to their culture.

I never felt uncomfortable wearing the traditional Pakistani clothing. I'm kinda paranoid that maybe they are judging me about the fact that I'm Muslim, and I just try to be the best person that I possibly can. I believe that you should treat everyone with respect, and that's what I try to do, I just try to be myself. But I do have a little bit of paranoia about people judging me just because I'm Muslim. When people hear that I'm Muslim, they always ask me, "How come you don't wear, you know, the head covering?" I just tell them it's a personal choice, you're not required to wear it. That's what I believe. You know, it takes a lot to cover your hair and do it every single day, because here your hair is kind of like your beauty. It takes a lot to do it. And not everyone can do it.

Going to a Catholic school is great because the Catholic religion is so much like Islam. The Old Testament is inside the Koran. All the stories about David and Isaac and Ishmael, they're all in the Koran, and so whenever I learn about Christianity, I also learn about my religion, too. And I learn about Judaism. And what's great about Christianity is that they talk about love so much and, like, it makes me want to be a better person. Like every time I go into religion class, I know I'm gonna learn something that'll make my faith stronger. Like my appreciation for people, my empathy for people will grow. We took this one class, Social Justice, that just makes me empathize for people. That's one of the main reasons why I want to be a writer and why I want to go out into third world countries and help others. Because everyone has those basic needs you need to fill. You know, whether it be love or food, clothing, and shelter. I just think everyone deserves that.

Trappings interview portrait,
Academy of St. Aloysius

Erika Soveranes

Santa Fe, New Mexico | July 2005

I'm going into eighth grade. I love to play soccer and I love any kind of music. I play with the Mariachi Conquistadors. I play three different instruments in the mariachi group. I play violin, guitar, and I'm taking up trumpet for mariachi. Outside of mariachi I play flute and piano. I've played flute since I was in the third or fourth grade, I've played piano since I was in fifth, and I started violin, guitar, and trumpet this year.

Mariachi consists of a lot of different instruments: guitarrón, guitar, violin, trumpet, and sometimes harps and flutes. And it's basically Spanish music, not like Spanish pop music, but a different type of Spanish music. I think it describes part of my heritage and just kind of who I am. It makes me feel powerful in a way because I feel I have the power to change the way American people look at music, like Spanish music and pop music, and stuff like that.

Well I shouldn't be talking, 'cause I like this kind of music myself, but people are too involved with, like, what's new, and what Britney Spears is doing next. I know this is kind of weird, but yeah, I kind of do like her. I think that could be a bad thing, but I'm not that involved with it like some people are. If

Trappings interview portrait, Georgia O'Keeffe Museum's O'Keeffe Art and Leadership Program for Girls

they're just focused on one type of music, they don't really get to know what other type of music is out there, and hey, they might even like that kind of music better than what they listen to now. And I feel that I can change that, I can bring mariachi music up to the surface and get it to come out in the open.

Power is like having the will to do something that you know you might not be able to do, but you still go ahead and try it anyway and you succeed at it. The first time I played my first musical instrument, the flute, I didn't really know how to play it. I had never played an instrument before, I was scared. And so I just tried it and I found out that I really loved it and so that kind of made me feel powerful.

La Cienega, New Mexico |
October 2006

Erika and Sativa Cruz performing
in La Cienega

I started high school this year. That's really fun. I'm in marching band and we're playing all kinds of music like Queen, Led Zeppelin, The Who, all kinds of stuff like that. We actually went to a pageant of the bands this year, and we won second place, people's choice, and best auxiliary. So we're all happy.

Music is practically my life. I revolve around music every day. I go to school and there's music. I come out of school, I have practice for music. Music could also be like a sanctuary, too. If I'm having a bad day, or if I don't like something that's going on, I'll pick up my flute or my guitar or my violin and I'll just play and play for hours. It gets me concentrating and just gets me away from it all.

Neeve

Carrboro, North Carolina | April 2003

I am a freelance worker and a drag king. This outfit makes me feel powerful because when I was eight years old, all I wanted to do was wear a cowboy shirt with cowboy boots. I was fortunate enough to have a mother who did let me wear those things, but I was unfortunate enough that none of the girls really seemed to be hot for me. So now, it's great because I get to wear it and I get appreciated for it.

I tend to get a little precise about my outfit. These boots are steel-toed. I consider that a bit of a hidden weapon, probably feel a little bit more secure with them on, just in terms of being able to kick a shin and then get out of there. These jeans I got in San Francisco—I think that's the only place to buy Levi's, personally. And I cut them just like my best friend cuts them. This belt—I got this in California—it says WE ARE NOT ALONE. It reminds me of that fact and keeps one eye toward the alien friends. And this shirt I got in my favorite city of all, Minneapolis. I've had gay men at conferences walk up to me and say, "That is the best cowboy shirt I've ever seen, I would buy it from you right now for like a hundred and fifty bucks." So, you know, in terms of like that culture and that aesthetic, I feel like it's a pretty good cowboy shirt.

In terms of my identity, sometimes if I dress like this with my very tight bra on, I can pass as a man, and that gives me power most

Trappings interview portrait,
Cuntry Kings headquarters

definitely, and definitely changes the way that I feel, unless I'm speaking. I have the awareness of being perceived as a straight white man. And that's the furthest thing from what I really want to be perceived as, just in terms of my sense of what that existence brings and what people bring to that existence, so I like to, you know, remind people that I'm a little faggy. Like to wear silver lip polish and, you know, glitter and stuff like that.

Presentation is just that, and we all do it every day, and we all can change the way that we do it, and we all can do it in a way that we never dreamed we would have been doing. That then changes how people interact with you. I learned that lesson. It's really frustrating for me because here I am, a person, a soul, looking to connect, looking to interact with people who aren't just like me. And they see me, and they smile at me, and they're really happy, and, you know, they think I'm a nice, kind young man. And then upon speaking, it's mainly just sort of dealing with their discomfort, you know? They become flustered. They apologize. Or they don't. That's a real thing between sort of the visual and the experience in terms of power. So I can take on power, but do I ever feel like I truly have it? No. Because I never feel like people are truly accepting me for who I am. At the same time, I feel like I am taking on a particular sort of power and a particular sort of wisdom because I'm able to see how people can interact with each other when it's really just a matter of two beings coming together, who aren't blinded by some sort of social consideration or religious consideration. But then I'm struggling with that because I'm still a white man. So I don't know. And I think that's why I play with it, you know? Because I think everybody should be playing with it. If people get that in their head, I think it could be a different situation in some ways.

Crystal Barrett

Memphis, Tennessee | October 2002

'm thirty-two, and I just begin to live my life for me, maybe two or three years ago. I'm a single mother of two boys. I have been in Memphis for four years. I have no family here. The only family I have is my Muslim family. This uniform I wear gives me power. I believe that it was designed by God, for me. And it was hard for me to accept it, I still have moments where I may not cover like I should. But when I wear this uniform, I receive so much respect, so many compliments, and I feel that I can accomplish anything.

I'm a Muslim, but I must say what type I am because, as of any church, is different Muslims. I'm in the Nation of Islam under the leadership of the Honorable Minister Louis Farrakhan. This is called an Imperial Uniform. This is the head-piece. This is the jacket. And we have a wrap skirt. It's really form as protection.

When I'm out in my garment, people, they know is something different about that woman. "Are you a nun?" That's the biggest question. Especially when I don't have my children. But even when I have my children, the question is still asked. So I explain, no, I'm not a nun, I'm a Muslim. Or, if it's ninety degrees outside, "I know you hot." No, because if you cover your skin from the sun it'll be more cool than if it's uncovered.

Trappings interview portrait,
Metropolitan Inter-Faith Association

The first time I put on a garment, I just can't explain how I felt. When I looked in the mirror it was like a transform of a different person. I just felt so different. And it just gives me power. I'm just loving Crystal. I'm able to feel like I can do what I want to do.

I love neutral colors, so this brown just does so much for me and my complexion. My children love my uniform. I have to tell my boys, "You don't mess with mommy headpiece," because that's something you never do. You don't mess with a sister's headpiece. But they really love who I am. And they accept me for me. And that's wonderful. It was hard for me to deal with the spiritual side of accepting that God actually chose me and this faith. But I am so happy, and I love this uniform.

I have an issue with speaking, like now, I'm nervous. But I pray to God that I get over that because I've seen a lot, I've done a lot, and I feel like I can help someone. Now I'm at a point, whoever I attract it's with my mind. It's nothing that they can see. And I get so many compliments. Even though I don't wear this uniform at work. I work at Federal Express. I wrap my hair, so they approach me. I know it's God. I know that. But for them to pick me out and say, you know, "Is something different about you?" You know, "Who are you?" And so that give me an incentive that I'm doing something right. I'm just so happy.

Sheelagh Cabalda

Jersey City, New Jersey | August 2004

What I wear that makes me feel powerful is a combination of two things. One of them is my ANGRY LITTLE ASIAN GIRL t-shirt. Wearing this shirt makes me feel powerful because I think that being a woman, being petite, and being Asian American, people, especially men, make certain assumptions about me. When I say or do something that shocks them, it catches them off guard, and I'd like to think that it makes folks think twice about what they think about Asian American women.

The other thing that makes me feel powerful is laughter, whether I'm doing the laughing or I'm making other people laugh. Laughter is such a powerful force because it totally makes me feel alive, whether I'm in a group or sitting alone and cracking myself up because I'm thinking of something. I cannot tell you the energy that I get from laughing. My dad always criticizes me, "Why do you have to laugh like that? That's too much, that's too big a laugh" and "That's not ladylike." I guess that's also connected to, like, why I wear t-shirts like this. I think that there's just something to be said for making people think, and I don't necessarily have to open my mouth all the time.

I think the power of shock and the power of provoking critical thinking and the power of laughter just creates an energy that enables people to interact and react to each other. And

Trappings interview portrait, Ria's Café

for me, as a person kind of going through this journey of life, interaction is really important. In another lifetime I would have loved to have been like the next Lucille Ball. If I have an opportunity to make somebody laugh, that just like gives me this surge and makes me feel really alive. There's just so much ugliness in the world, and it can get really depressing. If we can kind of insert some laughter, that creates also moments of peace. At least for me.

I work at the Asian Pacific American Studies Program at New York University. I've been there ten years. Interestingly enough, I didn't come into this diversity work because I wanted to. I saw that there were needs that weren't being met, and I play that role in helping students to request for those needs, and demand those needs. Now my passion is working with young people, high school students, getting them to explore their identities as young men, women, Asian American. And the sooner that can happen, the better, because we spend so much of our lives with this baggage behind us that it prevents us from being who we are. So whenever I wear a shirt in front of my students, they're always looking and they're like, "Okay, what is that?" Like, "Where did that come from? What does that mean?" It's also a great conversation starter.

I was on the PATH Train one time and I had this t-shirt on. This guy kept staring at me, and I knew he was staring at me, but I didn't say anything, and it wasn't until I was getting out he said, "Oh, I love your t-shirt. I need to get one for my girlfriend." And he happened to be this white man, so I assumed his girlfriend was Asian. In my circles there's always commentary on white men dating Asian women, which is fine, you know. There are many nice white men out there dating

Asian women. We're talking about stereotypes, you know, the stereotypes around Asian women that they're demure, that they're submissive, that they're really sexual and, you know, they'll do anything that a man wants them to do because it's just in their nature. I think that's why I wear shirts like this. There are very precise moments when we were growing up where it was like, "Good girls don't do that" or "Why are you doing that? That's not ladylike." "You're never gonna be married if you're behaving this way." So when I wear shirts like this, I'm saying, *I'm fine, this is who I am, take me or leave me, I don't care what you think. Because this is who I am.* And it didn't prevent me from finding someone who wants to marry me.

Vivian Swallow

Riverton, Wyoming | May 2006

My name is Vivian Swallow. My Indian name is Sunshine Woman. I'm a member of the Eastern Shoshone tribe. I'm also part English and Swedish. I currently work as a social worker at Indian Health Service in Fort Washakie, Wyoming. I attended school at Arizona State University, where I graduated with honors. I'm currently pursuing a master's degree in public health administration. I feel that education and learning is a lifelong process.

In addition to learning, I just love traveling. When I was in high school, I actually went for a year to Australia as an exchange student. I was able to interact with Aboriginal people and just all sorts of people. I was in the outback. They have a drum, and something similar to our Sun Dance, and I thought, *Wow, we're all the same,* although we do have some different beliefs. In '99 I went to Sweden, which was very exciting, because my father was a first-generation Swede. There I was also able to interact with the Sami, who are the people known as the Laplanders, they're the reindeer people. I also learned that

Trappings interview portrait,
Nita Kehoe-Gadway's home

they have a drum, they have different tribes, they have a structure similar to the teepee, they have their own language, and they eat dried reindeer meat. So there again, I thought, *Wow, we're all the same.* Because we have jerky, and we have the teepee, and it's just fascinating to travel and it empowers me as a person so that I can appreciate diversity.

Frequently on the reservation, because I am a breed, I encounter some difficulties because I am lighter. But I'm proud of who I am, and that's why I wear this dress. I'm an enrolled member and it makes me proud. At the same time, I'm also proud of my Caucasian background because they're very good people as well. In our tribe, and most other tribes, you are enrolled based upon blood quantum. It's a system that I think eventually will cause extinction of all tribes, not just our tribe. Some folks believe that the more Indian you are, you should have more power, and they oftentimes express that. I judge people just simply by their merits, not by whether they're four-fourths Indian or a fourth. But for some people it's very important. The way I've interpreted it is it's just sort of like Darwin's evolution, some sort of a survival tactic, which is equated to power. What power means to me is just having knowledge, being proud of who you are, regardless of what others might think. But essentially being able to embrace diversity, and just the knowledge and the willingness to share the knowledge with others.

I grew up in a small community here in Wyoming called Crow Heart, and we didn't have TV, we had radio, so we read a lot and used our imagination. I grew up on a ranch, and my dad always used to say, "Are you gonna herd these cows all your life or are you gonna get out there and do something?" I started school when I was very young, I was about four, and I graduated from high school when I was sixteen. My mom always made sure we had books. I was reading at a very young age. And my grandmother was a teacher, and she expressed how important it was to seek education and also that education and learning was lifelong.

My outfit is made out of elk hide. My mom taught me how to do beadwork. Everything that I'm wearing I've made, except for this ivory rose. There's different stitches when it comes to doing the beadwork. I have some lazy stitch, but most of my beading is tack work. That's something that's traditional to the Eastern Shoshone tribe. I have our rose. Originally the rose was sort of more like the wild rose. People from my mother's generation were sent to boarding schools where they learned how to sew, and so we adopted the more elaborate embroidery pattern for our roses. But the Shoshones are well known throughout the nation for our roses. I am also packing the wing of an eagle as well as wearing an eagle in my hair. The eagle is a very powerful symbol for Native Americans. And I'm wearing otter. Native Americans try to use stuff from nature because that's what they had to do to survive.

I always wear just a single feather because I'm single. I've never been married. And actually, there's a law that was passed by the United States where only Native Americans are allowed to have eagle feathers. It's against the law for anyone else. I earned my feathers through graduation and accomplishment. That wasn't something that was just given to me. I would wear this to powwows or the One Shot Antelope Hunt, and just for special occasions like that.

Vivian at the Arctic Circle

I have a travel bug. I don't know if that's because I'm part Viking or whatever, but I love to travel. When I get much older, I would like to settle here permanently 'cause I love Wyoming, but there's so much to the world that I haven't seen yet.

Debra Carrion

Jersey City, New Jersey | August 2004

I have four great kids. Two beautiful granddaughters. I'm taking care of them myself, helping my daughter raise my granddaughters. I have the twenty-five-year-old, I have a son that's in high school, and I got Amanda, she's thirteen, she's a bookworm. She's very smart. And then I have a seven-year-old, and that was my miracle baby, because if it wasn't for her, I wouldn't have known I had cancer in my uterus.

I'm in remission for three years now. They did testing when I was pregnant and they found it, and they wanted me to abort her and I couldn't do it. I was like almost six months, and people have their own choices, but I couldn't do that, and even if I'm struggling, I just couldn't do it.

I've been struggling for years. I was doing stuff on the side, you know, like babysitting, but it wasn't the same because it wasn't like a nine-to-five job. The kids would come home, "Oh, Mom, it's picture day." And I'm like, *Oh my God, I'm not working. How am I going to do this?* If I can't do for one, I won't do for all.

I took care of a lot of people. I was in the nursing field. This lady I was taking care of for three years, she died in Christ Hospital holding my hand. I was the only family she had. I just couldn't do it no more. I used to work for an agency, and

Trappings interview portrait,
Dress for Success

they had me going to these places where I had somebody put a gun to my head, and I was getting mugged in the elevator, and as much as I was bleeding through my nose, I still went up and cleaned myself up and took care of her, because there was nobody there to feed her. I went out on my own. I put some flyers in supermarkets, and I had three clients of my own. I would work with them during the day, and they didn't have much money. I mean I had this lady give me five dollars a day.

I like to help people. If you're cold and I have a jacket, I'll give it to you, 'cause that's the way I am, you know? I'm trying to teach my kids how to be that, and thank God they are.

Now I'm with Dress for Success and I love it. I volunteered with them for almost a year, and they liked the way I am with people, and the way I talk to people, and things I do. I love to see their reactions when they come in and they put that suit on, because I been there. I know how it is, and it feels so good to be dressed up, because I never could afford clothes like this. I used to always be in jeans and sneakers and looking for work. I never had the opportunity to be dressed up. Only on Christmas or my birthday. My kids now, they look at me and, "Mom, you're so beautiful!" It makes me cry, you know? It's a big difference. I sense them knowing that I'm trying to help them.

I'm a personal shopper. This is basically what I look like every day. I try to look professional, so I can have the girls look at me that way, and know that I know what I'm doing. I help them pick out a suit. I talk to them, see how they feel in that suit, and if they like it, then they take it. When they come out and you see that smile, you know you did something right, you know you did something with them. While *I'm* here you're not going to leave without anything.

I'm catching up on my bills because I freak out when I can't pay my bills on time. If my lights go off, my kids are going to be sitting in the dark. I can't go through that. You know, if it was me alone, I wouldn't care. If I only have enough to

Debra, making sure her clients don't leave without anything

feed them, I stay hungry. That's how I am. My kids will come first. They didn't ask to be born, I brought them into this world, and I have to take care of them because I don't have nobody else to help me with them. I'm still struggling, but it's getting better.

I was like in a hole for a while, and I couldn't understand why I couldn't get out of that hole. I couldn't get out of that hole for nothing. And when I was in the hospital for a few months, very sick, the doctors didn't think I was going to make it. I was getting skinnier and weaker. They told me I had fifteen months to live. I walked out one morning and I said, *You know what, I'm not ready to leave yet. There's a lot of stuff I have to take care of, and I can't put my kids through that.* So I just went through the surgeries, and some treatments, and I'm not ready to go yet. I'm really not.

Jersey City, New Jersey | October 2006

Debra at her new desk

I came from becoming a personal shopper to administrative assistant. I still do a little bit of personal shopper, when they need help. But now I schedule appointments, I fax referrals over, I greet people that come off the elevator, and I have a lot of responsibilities. It's a lot of work, but I enjoy it. I really do.

This promotion is much better. It's full-time, not part-time, making a little more money, and it's helping me focus on life 'cause I'm able to buy things for my kids now that I wasn't before. I still got my problems. I'm still struggling with certain things, but it's not as hard. Now I can go crazy shopping, but I gotta watch my money because my rent's higher. You know, the more money you make, the rent's higher. Before, I was able to look in the stores and wish I could buy certain things. Now I'm able to do it, eventually. It's a little easier, it's a little easier. You know, I feel good getting up and coming to work. I really do.

I always had that power in me. There was times I just didn't let it show so much. Now I feel like I have the power. You know, I got a lot of it now.

Stacey Devine

Jersey City, New Jersey | October 2004

I have a very, very unglamorous life, hence this outfit. My life has a lot of taking care of other people all the time. My father died before I was born; my mother was bipolar and she wasn't diagnosed until very late in life, so I spent a lot of time taking care of her. I gave birth to a son who is on the autistic spectrum. He is the biggest handful of a child I think I've ever encountered. Actually, I've seen worse now that I see where he goes to school. But my days are generally cleaning up two-pound coffee cans spilled over, cleaning up a big ol' jug of Aunt Jemima on the kitchen floor. This is all within thirty seconds of answering the phone or turning around.

I have not worked since he was born because he is very difficult. I haven't been able to find appropriate day care for him. I somehow manage to walk a tightrope very, very carefully of balancing who I really am and taking care of all these other people in my life. So the music that I listen to has really gotten me by all the things I've been dealing with in the past few years with my son, and during my teenage years, and with my mother. I can't play an instrument to save my life, but I sure do like hanging around people that come up with cool lyrics.

I did a little improv when I was living in Chicago. I wrote songs about being mentally ill. They were stupid songs like "Shut Up and Swallow Your Pills," and I produced shows there set in psych wards because that's a lot of

Trappings interview portrait,
Jersey City Museum

what I know. And interestingly enough, I decided to become a social worker to help even more people 'cause I just have so much time for myself that I feel like I just need to give everything else back to the world. So that was a very expensive private school tuition that I'm regretting. But, um, yeah, I'm making it and I feel good in this.

I'm always, always looking for vintage clothes. I ordered this off of a Web site that sells a lot of rockabilly clothes, and I know very little about rockabilly, but this was the dress for me. I just crossed my fingers, hit MEDIUM and SEND. And it fit like a glove.

This outfit really represents me being exactly who I am. This is an outfit that I wear to concerts for bands that I absolutely love. I wear something like this and no one in the world knows my story. I figure people actually probably make judgments based on what I'm wearing when I go to a concert, but I think they're all wrong, and it makes me feel powerful that they're wrong.

I think that people think that I'm single. I think people think that I'm younger. Sometimes guys hit on me even though I'm married and have children. I can wear this and I don't care what people think. Whereas if I were going to wear an outfit like this in the suburbs of Chicago, part of me just wants to say that I don't really care, but fact was, there was no one else around me that connected. No one liked music, no one had heard of anything other than Top 40 whatever, and all these mothers' lives were so focused on their children. I heard a quote, they all thought that the sun was shinning out of their sons' or daughters' asses. And I absolutely adore my kids, and I think Maddie, my nine-year-old, she's super cool and very well adjusted, and I think I'm doing as good a job as I can possibly be doing raising her. Not that other moms are wrong in the way that they choose to bring up their own children in more sheltered environments. I never wanted that for myself as a kid because I'd just seen so much chaos in my life and it made me a stronger person. So I think having my kids in an environment like New York City, it's going to make them stronger.

I just like the kids I'm raising although I have to do a lot of cleaning up.

And trust me, I'm not wearing this outfit when I'm cleaning things up. I'm wearing junky jeans, sweatshirts. And maybe once or twice a week I get to go to a concert and I get to dress up and I get to feel like myself. I feel like I'm walking that fine line and this is just the outfit of forgetting all of the bigger issues that I keep at home with me. This is just kind of like a fantasy outfit. My life is so unglamorous, and I feel just a tiny, tiny bit like a forties or fifties film star, and somehow that just makes me feel amazing. I'm glad that people misjudge my story when they look at me. I think it's really funny, and I think that people have a very set image on what a mother looks like and what a mother can be, and I feel like I'm doing a good job, but at least in my trappings I don't fit any kind of stereotype.

Caroline Honour

Albion, Michigan | March 2005

My mom is my biggest role model. You say you don't want to turn into your parents, but if I turned into her, it would be wonderful because she is such a strong person. When I feel bad, she is the one person who can talk to me and make me feel like it's all going to pass.

I was in my mom's old bedroom and I found this dress in her closet. She doesn't exactly remember what she wore it for. I remember wearing it when I graduated second in my class in high school. High school was a real bitch. I'm never going to go back. I'm not going back to my reunion. I'm not interested in anything that goes on there. It was a small town, three hundred kids in the high school, I only graduated with ninety. All white. No differences. Nothing was accepted and I didn't belong.

I gave a speech at graduation which really pissed a lot of people off, 'cause no one wants to hear me talk because of the way I feel. I turned in a fake speech to the principal because I knew I was going to say some things that he wasn't going to

Trappings interview portrait,
Trish Franzen's home

love. I talked a lot about how people in my high school thought high school was like *it* for them. It sounds almost cliché, but if you are the prom queen or if you are the captain of the football team, you've rose to be like all you can be because you made it in high school. And it's just like, the people who make it in high school, that are the kids who judge everyone else, are the ones who usually don't make it later on because they are cookie cutters, not the ones who are unique and gonna go places. The football captain ended up like failing out first semester, so it's almost like I called it.

It stormed on the day of graduation. Thunder and lightning and a downpour. It sort of suited the day. As I was saying a particular line in my speech

about how "high school is a shelter and we're going out into the world now, into the storm that's out there waiting for us." Coincidentally, I had to pause because it was thundering right as I was finishing that line. It was almost like I had commanded the weather.

I was wearing this dress beneath my gown. It was one moment that I felt truly most comfortable and most happy with myself. My mom has a huge family. We're Polish, so there was like thirty people there. They all really enjoyed it and made me give it at the house again afterwards. I've given it three or four times. I wanted to make sure I said everything I wanted. I didn't tell anybody what I was going to say the entire time before I graduated. I'd say, "Back off, I can't tell." And so everyone was completely surprised at graduation, but I feel like it was a good surprise.

Clara Lee at the Square

Clara Lee Arnold

Oxford, Mississippi | October 2002

I'm in training to be a professional boxer. Well, up until a few months ago I was the executive director of the Humane Society, which was my passion, and I loved it.

This is a small town and I know so many people, and when wind got out that I had done this, I would say 80 percent of the people were pretty much supportive, and had a real attitude like, you know, "Way to go." About 15 percent just thought I was just completely frickin' crazy. But they probably thought that about me already. And the other 5 percent would just look at me and go, "Why?" They didn't know what to think. My mother being one of those. It did take a lot of guts, but it felt really good. And my attitude has always been that life's real short and if you want to do something, then go for it.

I've always been fascinated with things that mentally and physically and emotionally challenge you. And boxing does all of those things. It's by far the most physically, emotionally challenging thing I have ever done. It takes every bit of wherewithal you have to get in the ring. I went from having an income to poverty, but, you know, all the good boxers were poor.

I've got until I'm thirty-five to turn pro. I'm an ex–professional tennis player, professional sports is not something new to me. I have yet again picked a professional sport where I have to travel to train. There is nobody I can train with in Oxford, Mississippi. I have to drive to Memphis to do it. Mostly I have to spar with men, who I actually kind of have a problem sparring with. They have problems really letting go until I get a coupla good shots in, and they get a little braver.

Trappings interview portrait, Oxford Public Library

I think that most guys are still holding back. I box at the Memphis Police Boxing Gym. These guys are boxers, so they do understand that they have to give me a fight. It takes a lot getting past hitting someone and getting hit. I remember the very first time I got a really good shot in on my trainer. I stopped. His nose is bleeding, and I'm, "Oh, so sorry." And he's like, "That's the sport. You got to get past that part." You got to be able to see the blood and then really move in for the kill. So it takes a mental switch that you have to go through. And the same thing with being hit. I have people ask me all the time, "Why do you want to be hit?" Well, I don't want to be hit. When I get hit, what registers with me is *Oh, I made this mistake.* Not *Gee, that hurt.* You don't focus on the pain when you're in the ring.

One of my hangups has always been I have never felt like a real feminine woman. This is really helping, I know. When I tell that to people, they look at me and go, "You are one of the most feminine women I know." That's because I'm overcompensating. I buy the flowered-y dresses for a reason. My mother said, "You're never gonna get a date as long as you are a boxer." Well, she also told me I was not going to get a date until I lost ten pounds either. Um, anyway, that's a whole other issue.

Round Two. Ding. I feel just as powerful in this as I do my boxing gear. I have an evening gown collection. I don't know what it is, but put me in a long dress and a pair of heels and I feel like I can take on the world.

Part of my former life as the executive director of the Humane Society was we threw events and fund-raisers and all that kind of stuff. I was always the hostess. So many people dislike dressing up, and I love it. I mean any opportunity. I will drive, you know, a hundred miles if I think there is an opportunity to wear a long dress. I don't care what the event is. Wear a gown? Great. I'm there. I haven't gone so far as to wear this kind of stuff to Wal-Mart, but I'm thinking about it after this.

A whole other power outfit. I do have a lot of lingerie.

I feel really powerful in my lingerie, and I'm sure it has partly to do with that whole feminine thing again. I try so hard to be feminine and look feminine because deep down inside I feel like a linebacker. So I picked one of my little lacey, frilly, cutesy things. That hopefully, given wearing it in front of the right person, will make me the most powerful creature on the earth.

I think that what makes me feel powerful are my voice and my physical strength. I think there is some kind of conflict in there, too, because I am very strong, and I have a very aggressive personality, very authoritative. I don't mind walking into a group of people I don't know, and if nobody else is going to take charge, I'll be glad to. The hangup with that is I am turning thirty-four, and I am still single, and my mom keeps telling me I'm never gonna get a date.

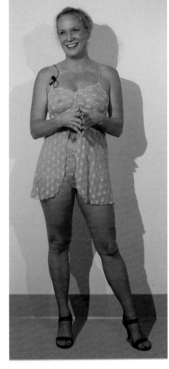

But I tell you what, I leave Oxford, Mississippi, and I feel like a babe. I really do. I was dating a man in Columbia, Missouri, for a while, and I would go up there and I was like, *Oh man, I look good.* There is just an attitude in Oxford to be looking great all the time. I'd go to the grocery store in Missouri and I'd have on makeup. And people would be looking like, Why are you so dressed up for the grocery store?

I grew up here, but I'm certainly not the little typical Oxford woman that is very meek and mild and pretty and Southern and has a clean house, and has the right husband. Of course I'm generalizing, and I'm not poking fun at any particular person. But we're very proud to be Southern here. And I'm not the typical Southern Belle at all. And I think there is part of me that wants to be, and there is part of me that's proud I'm not. So it's a constant struggle.

Oxford, Mississippi | March 2006

I've got dresses everywhere. I've got throws that I love. Fancy skirts. As you can tell, the whole room is a closet. Golden ponchos and pashmina cashmere scarves. I cannot ever remember dressing up as a kid. I was such a little tomboy and was always in shorts and t-shirts and probably dirty half the time or on the tennis court. I didn't enjoy dressing up then. I found a lot of contradictions between my childhood and my adulthood.

As I think I told you before, I kind of always struggled with my masculine side and my feminine side. You know what? I feel more feminine than I ever have in my life. And I think emotionally, I'm in a really good place right now. I just feel very confident about myself, and what I'm doing, and where I'm going—I can't say it never bothers me, otherwise I wouldn't have a closet like this. I enjoyed the boxing, but not boxing probably helped that.

I didn't turn pro. There were lots of factors in that, but I would say the biggest factor was my mother. She was in not great health the year that I turned thirty-five. I knew that she really didn't like me boxing. I would have to say that another part of it was, I've lived in Oxford all of my life, and it was a just little scary to think about up and moving and going somewhere. And I'd already had my jaw broken once and my nose broken three times, which I got fixed this past summer. It really doesn't look all that different, but I can breathe on both sides, that's the good news. So I just channeled that energy somewhere else.

For the last four years I've been giving boxing lessons. I have worked with men and women. At the moment, I'm training Myrna Colley-Lee. Her husband is Morgan Freeman, which, ironically, he won an Oscar for a boxing movie. So when I asked him if he would please purchase her a heavy bag and gloves for her birthday a few weeks ago, he looked at me like I was crazy, but he did and she loves it. I've never put the gloves on anybody that doesn't love it. I do miss it sometimes, and I think that is why I created my boot camp class.

I am kind of known as the hardcore, kick-ass instructor at the fitness center. So if someone comes in wanting a trainer that's really gonna kick their butt, they immediately get forwarded to me. We've been talking about having t-shirts made up that say CLARA LEE IS KILLING ME, but I don't know if the owner's actually gonna let us do that. I think everyone in my class would actually purchase one, though.

I have thought about y'all several times over the last few years. Every once

in a while, a friend would Google me and would come up with the pictures. I had a friend that lived in Indianapolis and he sent me this just glowing e-mail about, "Hey, I found your pictures online and I was just thinkin' about you and there you were! And I listened to your interview and isn't that neat?"

And then I was aware that a few years ago, someone had sent out pictures of me in an e-mail. It's just, it's too small a town, and also the Internet makes it a much smaller world, and so eventually it got around to me that someone was saying derogatory things about me and these pictures. And, um, a few years later those pictures came up in a divorce court case that I was a witness for, and one of the attorneys pulled up the pictures that he had copied off of the Internet, in essence insinuating that a person that would have pictures like this of themselves on the Internet was essentially putting themselves out there and trolling for men. 'Course if you tell anybody that you've got pictures of yourself on the Internet, that immediately sounds bad. There have been too many Paris Hilton videos and Pamela Anderson videos out there. Despite any explanation that I had, trying to explain the project, they were taken as illicit pictures. And that was upsetting, but at the same time, I certainly don't regret doing the project. I'm just not a person that's full of regrets for things that I have done. I had a lot of positive reinforcement before that instance about the photographs. Now I kind of look back on that and say, Well, small-minded people can make a big deal out of very unimportant things.

And while I feel like I'm in an even better place than I was four years ago, and mentally

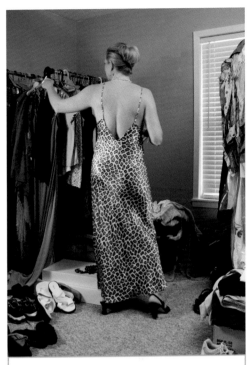

Not every girl in town has such a walk-in closet.

stronger, and more emotionally self-assured, I'd pretty much wear the same things. I just got back from a cruise. Even on a casual day, I felt more formal. My shorts were pressed, my tank top had no wrinkles in it, my hair was neatly braided. And then for the formal nights, I had on a formal dress, long gown, usually slit up the side, the proper evening bag, the correct jewelry. And there were people from literally all over the world on this cruise. I got a lot of questions and a lot of very nice compliments, which certainly all of us want. So, yes, I still feel like when I leave Oxford, I'm a babe!

Penny Henry

Kansas City, Missouri | June 2005

Power for me has come with age. I grew up in a very small town. I counted at least nine, maybe eleven, churches in a town of three thousand. We had possibly six African American people who were over sixty-five, and that was the diversity that I grew up with. There were Democrats and Republicans and there were Catholics and Protestants, but there was no other diversity at all. So power to me came with age. I was someone's daughter, I was someone's wife, and I was someone's mother until I left the small town at the age of fifty and moved to the big city and became myself. While I don't have a feeling of power over anyone else, I feel comfortable in my skin, which gives me power to not be overpowered by other people, although if I had better clothes, I could handle that better.

When I'm at work, all the very young children that work there just treat me with respect, not because I'm so old and in my dotage, but I don't get in their hair and I don't get in their way. I seem to be on the same level with them, and I've never felt that way with people my own age that might be threatening to me. Because of my seniority in years and seniority in my position, I feel powerful, just comfortable and powerful. Power over myself to exist and have my own thoughts of what is right and how the

Trappings interview portrait,
Cinna Turnbull's home

world ought to be. And if you don't agree with me, that's your problem. Where before I've been more milk-toasty about it.

Kansas City isn't that far from where I grew up. Seventy miles. And from seventy miles away, it looked like the epitome of sophistication and culture. And you could shop. Where I come from, there are no longer clothing stores. The movie theater burned down. There are tractor pulls and softball games, and so I moved to the city to be able to partake in culture.

My parents were prominent citizens of the community; they were newspaper publishers. I was one of three daughters. I was the one that stayed in the area to care for my aged parents. My aged parents up and died on me and there was really no reason to stay, because my children had grown and gone. I had an ex-husband who had a very young, good-looking wife who lived in town. There was really no reason for me to stay there. All the stars aligned. So I moved to the big city.

Not only did I grow up in a *Leave It to Beaver* family, but everyone I knew grew up in a *Leave It to Beaver* family. And here, I don't think I've run into half a dozen people that came from that kind of family background. I work with gays and straights. I work with people from India and people from Europe and from all over the world. I work with some radical right-wing people. I can declare that I'm no longer radical right-wing, although I've been there and lived fifty years that way.

It was just liberating when you actually confront the fact that you have a gay child. You grew up knowing that those people were evil and awful, lurked in public rest rooms in trench coats. I realized that my child didn't even have a trench coat and didn't do a lot of lurking. I don't know how I came to that perception, it just kind of was just in me. But if I was that wrong about that, I might possibly be wrong in some of the other things that I had accepted as fact all my life.

I always suspected that he was gay. From when he was a very small baby, I suspected he was different, but if you don't address those things, maybe they won't be true, and people tend to live up to what you expect of them, and nothing can be lower than expecting them to be gay, so I would expect him to be straight and not mention it to him because it wouldn't occur to him to be. But it did occur to him to be, and through an accidental conversation with my other son I mentioned I didn't even know for sure that son number two was gay. And son number one said, "Of course he's gay!" Then we addressed it. And since then, it's been a learning process and he's been very, very, patient with me. He's been helpful to teach me that it was because I wouldn't let him play with Barbie dolls, I'd only let him play with Kens and GI Joes, so of course he got this attachment for boys.

We've just been very, very close. And it's fun. When I went to California and I needed some makeup, my son could say, "Here, Mom, I'll get you mine." That was fun. A friend of mine has just been diagnosed with Hodgkin's, and she is going to have chemo, and she is going to lose her hair. Well, this same son has offered some of his wigs.

When I moved to the city, I had to reexamine everything. Everything. And it was a hard few years while I did that, but it's been very liberating. I'm still a registered Republican. I just want to screw up the primaries. My best friends from my hometown are still my best friends, but I don't get to spend as much time with them as I'd like to. I've come to know people who have a much broader worldview, and just the diversity, it's just wonderful. It's like going from Wonder white bread to seven-grain bread.

Bille Wickre

Albion, Michigan | March 2005

I've been thinking a lot about why women are so reluctant to claim power or to speak of power. Even the word seems to be a problem. Something that has kind of been running through my head is just this phrase about *speaking truth to power.* If we claim to *be* power, then who will speak the truth? And what does it mean if we *are* power? What responsibility does that give us? And I just can't sort of get out of that loop. I think women for so long have been disempowered, or on the unfortunate side of power. So it's really hard for us to make that transition.

I feel this strongly in my own life because I grew up in a family in rural South Dakota. We were very, very poor and neither of my parents finished high school. I was the first one in my family, ever, to go to college. And I've always felt very much outside of, and unfamiliar in, an academic atmosphere and an atmosphere where most of my peers are middle class and sometimes more than that. I think for me dressing is about creating a character that I can step into. And I can be that character no matter how I feel behind that façade, in spite of that masquerade.

My wardrobe sort of has three levels of characters. There's the character that's on the floor playing with the dogs. And that's the character that feels courageous, the character that does animal rescue, it's the character that goes to the humane society, it's the character that goes out in the middle of the night and does sexual assault counseling. And then there's the sort of casual professor, like out and about on campus, and, you know, just talking to students and trying to be cool. And then there's the professional. Which is, you know, the top layer. I teach art history.

One thing that I think is power is this jacket because it feels to me like protection. It's not quite like a talisman; it's an object of clothing that I wear that makes me feel safe and courageous. I think that a lot of courage, for me, grows out of outrage. And that gives me courage to do things that I wouldn't normally feel like I could do.

A lot of the things I do are about protecting the powerless. I think any change that any of us make in the world brings everyone along. And so, if we model compassion or if we soothe the pain or the suffering of another creature, I think we bring the world along. I think we just make everything better. And we make ourselves better in doing it.

I seem to have some affinity for dogs. One of my friends said that if my genetic makeup were explored more fully, they would find that I was part dog. Even in my very best being-a-professional outfit, I am covered in dog hair. Somebody's always pulling a wad of fur off me, which kind of undoes the whole look. It makes it less compromising to me personally. Which I realize is a complicated

and weird thing to say, but given my background and sort of who I feel I am inside, playing this role, or what after many years still feels like a role, in many ways feels like a betrayal of where I came from, and where my family still is. And so there is a compromise in playing the role that is sometimes very costly, and anything that kind of undoes the perfection of the role can allow that compromise to be undone a little bit and can allow less feeling of betrayal.

This is so complicated, this idea of power and clothing and presentation. Like, the first day of school takes me forever to get dressed. 'Cause I have to be that professor who I don't feel like, and I have to command a presence. Sometimes, I go to my closet and it's not like I'm picking clothing. It's like I have a cast of characters living in there. And I'm picking *Who am I gonna be today?* So I'll dress to present myself and I have the posture and the voice. I'm still often standing in front of the class every single first day of class, and I'm ssshaking and I'm hhholding on and I'm hhhoping my voice will get a little more steady. And you know, I'm thinking, *These are eighteen-*

Trappings interview portrait, Lynne Chytilo's home

207

year-old students, what am I in a panic about? And I think it's just always this kind of sense of being a fraud or being discovered or that somehow the ground is just gonna fade away.

I brought the outfit that, for me, right now, is my I'm-very-cool-with-who-I-am outfit. This is what I wear when I want to make other people think I'm powerful, which doesn't necessarily mean that it always makes me feel powerful. But sometimes it does. I think it's kind of like being happy. If you project happy, then sometimes you pull yourself along. Other people are maybe perceiving power, and you can see it's not hurting them, or it's not endangering your relationship with them, and so you can start to feel more comfortable with it.

Mostly my family ignores it, or sometimes denigrates it. You know, "You're

not such a big deal" or "I don't know why you couldn't have been something else." Which is what I hear a lot in my family. Two summers ago, I went home, and my cousin, with whom I was very close when we were children, we were just sitting at the table together and she said, "You know, you made it out." And that was very touching. It was very moving to me, and, um, that wasn't at all about power, but I felt very empowered by it. I felt kind of accepted and encouraged by at least one person in my family. So that was good. That was a good thing.

It would be great to have some kind of organization on campus that would provide a forum for discussion of just this kind of distancing and identity and the kinds of issues that people experience if they come into this quite foreign terrain. I mean, how do you even know how to apply to college, and how do you even know to go to college? Which I think is, you know, a really big thing. Really big. And then how do you deal when you're there and beyond?

Dorothy Allison has a great essay

about what it's like to grow up poor, and she talks about the shame of it and the shame of always hiding your family and hiding your background and never feeling good enough. And I think it's kind of an unnamed shame. It's not about anything you've done. It's about who you are and who you're made to believe you are. I remember growing up—and this is still very much with me—being accused of being lazy all the time because I was poor. Today I feel lazy all the time. I feel like I could be working hard, or I could be accomplishing, or I could be doing this, I wanna do more, and I need to do more, and if I let down at all it'll be true. I will be lazy, or I will be stupid, or someone will know that I'm awful. I think a lot of people probably feel bad in a lot of different circumstances. But we have a weird country where this happens. I don't know why. You know, politically we need to get together. Right? And I guess that's why I do everything I do. That's why I teach the classes I teach. That's why I teach about political art and women's art and all that stuff.

Amelia M. Joiner

Pittsburgh, Pennsylvania | January 2005

Well, my name is Amelia Michele Joiner. To my friends, Michele. To the people I work with, Amelia Joiner.

I knew ever since I was three or four that I wanted to be a lawyer. It's not exactly what I thought. It's not at all what I thought. I thought I would be helping people and righting wrongs. Not exactly what I do.

I will never be happy in Corporate America. I'll do it and I'll do okay at it. I might even do well, but it's not my passion. It's not what I love, it's not what makes me feel good about myself when I look in the mirror. Coming from my background, we were just poor, straight poor, and working for corporations to me is just almost a sense of betrayal. I don't feel like I'm using the gifts I have been given to help those that really need it. I don't think Corporate America needs me. They don't deserve me. But it's what I have to do to make sure my children have the options to do Corporate America if they so choose. If you choose to do neighborhood legal services or political activism or you want to do something that is far less appreciated, then that's fine. That's great, too. But I want you to choose, and I want you to get out. I want you to have the options. And so I have to pay the price now.

This is my power suit. It's called the Power Navy, and I have the Power Pearls on as well. It's powerful to me because when I was little the people who wore suits were always the very important people. As I got older, that just never changed. When I got into law school it was, okay, you can have on any old suit if you want to, but you *need* to wear a suit that commands respect but is not too harsh. That's why for me, it's the Power Navy and not the power black, and certainly not the power tan.

I got the whole black woman thing, where you're not supposed to be there. But I'm also a big woman. I'm tall and I'm big. But with the Power Navy, I mean, it just doesn't matter. It doesn't matter that I'm big, it wouldn't matter if I was small, when I put on a Power Navy suit, like, I am just the boss of somebody. And I know something. I think it really exudes power. And you have to have a good bag, and I have a very, very good bag that goes with the Power Navy suit. It's the Power Navy Prada.

That bag is really not to be played with. It's got white piping around here, and that good shoe has that white piping. You see what I'm saying? That's not to be played with. You can't just run out and get you a Prada. You can not. You have to be somebody to rock this shoe and this purse and the good Power Navy suit. Where you going? Where you going? You gotta be going somewhere. That's why I feel like this is powerful. 'Cause you can't just be slumming around. You can't go to the grocery store in your Power Navy, you know? You have to be going somewhere up.

I think my life has changed so much, so quickly that I haven't even had the opportunity to really learn who I am, let alone where it is that I'm powerful. I do not feel powerful at work. I'm very uncomfortable there. I'll smile nice and I work and play well with others, but I do not feel that I'm powerful there because I don't think I fit.

That's why I say the whole being of a large law firm is just a very unhealthy place for your mental state. If you really don't get yourself right, and you don't feel very confident and very strong, those people can drive you crazy, straight crazy. Because you're always feeling like you're trying to fit. I've been down that path, trying to be who they are. You get to the point where it's like, *Now I'm one of them, but I don't like them.* It stands to reason that then you don't even like yourself.

That's what I do and that's my job, but I feel most powerful and most at ease with my children and my husband. I'm most comfortable with those people and I feel very powerful there because I feel like I'm appreciated, I'm understood. I feel very loved. I feel like it's okay for me to be me.

Trappings interview portrait,
Rana Wright's home

Amelia at work; Amelia Michele's interview; Michele with the twins

So, my family calls me Michele. The people who feel closest to me call me Michele, because if I'm allowing you to call me Michele, I've kinda let you come into family. And you're kind of in a whole other world. But at work, most people know me as Amelia because you really just have to stay out. You don't belong in and that's kind of it. It's two different people, and it's a shame but everyone does it. I just actually have names for it. I'm Amelia Joiner or I'm just Michele.

The people in Michele's world don't respect the Power Navy suit. They could care less about the Power Navy. They care about that good bag, though. Michele, for me, would be in a good pair of jeans with some shirt that shows cleavage. I have really good cleavage. I mean, it's superb. Most of my body I do not like, but the twins are all right. So, you know, I will put on the cleavage-enhancing bra and gloss the girls up. And that's a lot of power right there. I'm big, and I'm tall, but I will still put on a three-inch heel, boot or shoe, and rock it. And just have to look down to everyone. In a good pair of jeans and a good, good, good foot, that bag, and that shirt with the girls all glossed up, that's all right. This is Amelia. But I mean, you know, it's two entirely different people. Completely.

Pittsburgh, Pennsylvania | October 2006

In law school, we had this notion that the really smart people were at the top of the class and they automatically chose to go to large law firms. The people who were a little bit less smart, well, they went to the medium-sized firms, then the smaller firms, and then ultimately you just had these *others*. They went to work for the district attorney, and finally neighborhood legal services. So I discounted the attorneys there and their ability, which is sad to say. And I should be ashamed of myself, but I think a lot of people feel that way.

Neighborhood legal services was the absolute best professional experience I've ever had. I've worked at two large law firms, and when I got there I realized that the attorneys there were the best in the city. I thought, *Okay, I was all wrong, even I had a prejudice.* They actually cared about their clients. It wasn't that they cared that the client was gonna get ticked off at them and yell at them, they cared because they were people and had this great cause for which they were fighting, even when it was a loser.

Coming from the background that I came from, we often didn't have anyone to fight for us. I could identify very easily with most of our clients. I was very comfortable with them because they were very much like me, the *me* that I am when I'm at home, because that's the *me* that I grew up. It was easy to work very long hours, to work very hard, to fight for them.

It was a wonderful, wonderful opportunity. And I absolutely hated to leave. Because it was very rewarding and I felt good about what I did. I never came out of there feeling like *I won the case, but I do feel dirty.* Those people, they needed you, and they were very grateful, and so it was just the best experience. You had to be a very good attorney because you didn't have the luxury of asking a senior-level associate, a partner, the expert in the field. You had to be the expert and you had to represent your client, and a lot of times their livelihood depended on whether you did a good job or not.

When I was there, I had a passion. I really believed in my clients. And when you have a passion you can get angry. It's kind of that fire in the belly that you feel when you're in law school, when you have a passion to learn, and the people with the fire are the ones who do the best.

It's unfortunate that no one gives them more money so that they can have the resources to do a better job. Lawyers like me, how I used to be, we discount them, so we come in and we're very prepared and we're ready to kill you. They just casually stroll in, and they're not in the perfect Power Navy, they just come in looking like anything, and oftentimes looking like hell. And they come in and then they just beat the crap out of you. And it's the greatest thing ever because this is one of the few times where the low man actually beats the person who has all the money and power. I think it's fabulous.

I tried this case in federal court. It's all the talk of the courthouse now. My client was a convicted first-degree murderer, and he is serving a life sentence at one of the state correctional institutes in Pennsylvania. While he was there

Amelia in front of the federal courthouse

he was involved in, admittedly involved in, some shenanigans where he got into a prison fight in the prison yard. The guy against whom he was fighting comes up to him with a knife in his hand, stabs my client in the back. We sued for violations of the Eighth Amendment because he has a right to be protected, and they have a duty to protect him as prison guards.

In 2001, the number of women surpassed the number of men enrolled in law school. When Amelia Michele Joiner graduated from Duquesne University in 2002, she was the only African American in her class.

I think we sent a message. We really went after the prison guards. My client actually thanked me for making one or two of the prison guards turn red, start sweating, and shake on the stand. We tried a wonderful case. It was clear that we would have never won the case. But we let the prison know, and we let the state know, that if you continue to engage in this type of behavior, some little cowboy like me will come after you. And that's what we did.

I'm gone from the firm and I am clerking for a federal judge in the Western District of Pennsylvania, Judge Joyce Flowers Conti. I will be sitting in on every trial, every motion, every status conference, every settlement negotiation, everything that the judge does. Afterwards I do the research, and then together we come up with the right decision.

The Power Navy has not been there. There has been no need for her, I think. Because of my experiences, I already feel kind of empowered. And so I don't necessarily need the Power Navy to hold on to anymore. Maybe something will come up. I might have to wear it when I write this really awful opinion that I have to write this week, but for the most part, I feel the power all by myself, so I don't necessarily need the clothes anymore. I got 'em, though. I still have my good bag. The pearls—I can't let 'em go.

Cecile Springer

I have a story to tell. And the story that I have to tell is one that I've come to love as I understand how important it is to know who you are and where you are.

I've lived in Pittsburgh for forty-six years, but I still consider myself to be a New Yorker. It's one of those things that just don't grow out of you. My parents are both immigrants to the United States. My mother came from Barbados, so she was very British, and my father came from Panama. Because of the culture of their countries, education was primary. In Barbados, everyone is literate. We were expected to be number one, and we worked at it.

My mother-in-law is an internationally known labor union representative. And one day I get a call from her and she says, "Cecile, I have something for you." And I said, "Oh really?" She said, "The first time you have an opportunity to come over to see me, come so I can give you this gift." When I get to see her, she's seated down very calmly, and she has something in her lap. And in her lap is a jewelry box. And I said, *Isn't that interesting? I wonder what she is going to give me.* And it turned out to be a piece of jewelry that's a rose.

And this rose is a transforming rose. I change every time I put it on. I become happier, and I'm very proud of the fact that I'm wearing something that someone gave me because she loved me enough to give it to me. And it's so important to me because the female part is the diamond, and these little rubies around represent how a rose gets together.

It is a beautiful piece and it makes a statement for her to give it to me. Every time there's some big event and my mother-in-law happens to be with us, I'm always wearing it. And I can see her smiling and saying, "Cecile really enjoys the pin."

When I was working, I traveled a lot to speak on lots of subjects. Some of the subjects were on leadership for women; some were very technical, 'cause I was in nuclear at the time, so I was always talking about nuclear energy and how safe it was and how important it was and how effective it was, etcetera. And I often would wear this pin because for me it transformed me into not

Trappings interview portrait,
Cecile's home

only a powerful person but an articulate person. And it's amazing to me that some object could do that, but it provides one with an inner sense of value.

I would define power as having the ability to make a decision, have it carried out, and be able to measure the outcome. I measure everything that I do. I come up with a calendar in a day, and if I haven't accomplished something in that day, then I am not satisfied. I shouldn't have a day to waste. I have too many things to do. Power is being able to do that, and be able to measure it, and know that it made an impact.

A women's organization had asked me, from Pittsburgh, to go to Iowa to be the main speaker at a luncheon. And I remember not having a sense of what the environment was like. Coming from New York, Iowa has green grass growing and farms with wheat, that's my perception. When I got there, I was being introduced to some of the women. One woman owned a gas line between Alaska and Texas. Another one had a trucking firm. Another one owned a school. A number of the women were in real estate. This was not a business group, it was a group of women leaders. And fortunately for me, what I had decided to do was to talk about leadership. What was leadership? How do you express it? Who are leaders and what happens as a result? The person who preceded me was a senator from her state to the Congress. And I was saying, *Oh my goodness, she's a senator and she's gonna precede me, what am I going to do?* Well, it turned out that she had a political statement to say and I had a leadership statement to say.

My statement was essentially women should take charge of their lives. There are elements of leadership skills that one has to know. You have to be able to communicate. You have to be able to show that you have something that people want to follow you about. We all can make powerful statements, do powerful things, and really struggle to make sure that what we do other people can follow.

And I remember speaking, and the room went silent. You're at a luncheon, and when a room goes silent, something is happening. I'm talking and looking and trying to figure out what was going on. And after I spoke, nothing happened. And everybody rose and gave me a standing ovation. I almost cried. I'm almost crying now. To think that they actually heard what I had to say was so powerful. It was just a wonderful event for me. And I wore my pin.

ALTERNATIVE ARRANGEMENTS FOR *TRAPPINGS*

CLOTHING ITEMS

Adornments

Colors

Cultural Emblems

Party Outfits

Shoes

The Stage

NOTES AND CREDITS

All photographs and texts in this book are by Two Girls Working unless noted.

Page 7, Photo of Claire Yannacone courtesy of her shipmate Kristin Ellison.

Page 8, Photo of the *Picton Castle* © Winward Isles Sailing Ship Co., Photo by Daniel Moreland. Used with permission.

Page 10, Photo of Betty Friedan, 1960, *New York World-Telegram* and *The Sun Newspaper* Photograph Collection (Library of Congress).

Page 10, Photo of Phyllis Schlafly provided by Eagle Forum.

Page 11, *Equality of rights under the law shall not be denied or abridged by the United States or by any state on account of sex*, Section 3 of the Equal Rights Amendment, written by Alice Paul in 1923.

Page 26, Photo of Anne Barry in her studio by Daniel Lovering.

Page 40, Photo of Linda Davis in her gallery courtesy of her daughter.

Page 42, Photo of Tina, Maida, and Sonia courtesy of Tina Camero.

Page 44, Studio and installation photos by Laura C. Hewitt.

Page 45, Photo of Laura hunting by Keith A. Hewitt Jr.

Page 58, Photo of Marcia Blacksmith by Brian Fraker.

Page 62, Photo of *Eggs on End: Standing on Ceremony* by Pillar de la Tierra courtesy of Donna Henes.

Page 68, Photo of Vivian Goldstein and Mary Rosenberg courtesy of Heather Arnet.

Page 69, Photo of suffragettes, George Grantham Bain Collection (Library of Congress).

Page 94, Photo of Caresse Crosby, née Mary Phelps Jacob, *The Passionate Years* by Caresse Crosby, Ecco Press, 1979.

Page 94, Image of the bra designed by Mary Phelps Jacob, from *The Passionate Years* by Caresse Crosby, Ecco Press, 1979. Patent in the collection of the U.S. Patent Office.

Page 95, Peggy Shumaker's "Turquoise Dress" first appeared in *Ascent*, Summer 2004. It was reprinted in *Just Breathe Normally*, University of Nebraska Press, 2007. Used by permission of the author.

Page 100, Photo of Beth and Kim Hafner courtesy of Renee Piechocki.

Page 123, Photo of Tara with her grandmother and mother courtesy of Tara McComb.

Page 126 Photo of Rocio and Mary courtesy of Rocio Aranda-Alvarado.

Page 147, Information about Title IX from the National Women's Law Center.

Page 186, Photo of Vivian at the Arctic Circle courtesy of Vivian Swallow.

Page 195, Photo of Caroline Honour at her graduation courtesy of Caroline Honour.

NAMES OF TRAPPINGS PARTICIPANTS, 2001–2006

Note: When women attend a *Trappings* interview session, they may choose not to be interviewed. The list below includes everyone who attended sessions.

* Interview session host or organizer

Carolyn Aanestad
Helen Aarli
Elaine Abadie*
Susan Abnos
Ashley Adams
AHM
Elizabeth Albin
Valerie A. Alchier
Gillian Alessio
Rachel Allenger
Terri L. Allred
Judith Antell*
Rocio Aranda-Alvarado*
Armi
Heather Arnet*
Clara Lee Arnold
Kari L. Aspaas
Ann L. Avery*
Mahtab Ayatollahi
Bianca B.
Gwen Bagley
Kim Baker
Victoria Baker
Christine Balance
Rebecca Barbee
Crystal Barrett
Anne Barry
Amelia Barton
Valerie C. Basnight
Marilyn Batts
Linda B. Becker
Cathie Behrend*
Leila Be-Na-Majenu
Pamela Bennett
Ciel Bergman
Suzanne H. Bertolett

Sarah Bilbao*
Georgia Binnington
Marcia B. Blacksmith
Molly Blieden
Christine Bodwitch
Georgia Boley
Ellen Borges
Kimberly A. Botza
Mary L. Bou
Amanda Boundy
Norma Sanders Bourdeaux
Vanessa Bowman-Allen
Sejal Brahmbhatt
Marion Jones Brooks
Lourdes S. Buencamino
Herschell Bugg
Kassie Bull Tail
Nancy P. Burnham*
Veronica A. Burress
Sheelagh Cabalda*
Rizalina Cabalda
Susan Cahill
Tina Camero
Courtnay Campbell
Susan Cannon
Pat Cappeto
Heidi Card*
Debra Carrion
Louise Carter
Erin Casey
Shuly Cawood
Susan Chin
Kirsten Christopher-Clark
Lynne Chytilo*
Rachel Citron
Jamie Clarke*

Laura Coats
Helen Cohen*
Joyce Cohen*
Niya S. Cole
Dinerra Coles
Jennifer L. Collins
Fialeli Colon*
Juana Colon
Natalie Colón
Cyndi Conn
Mary Ann Conway
Laurie Cooper
Lillian Corti
Jamilla Counts
Aretha Cozma
Dorothy B. Crabb*
Margaret Craddock
Jennifer Craft
Pam Cravez
Emily D. Crichton
Weatherly Crosland
Rachel Crutchfield*
Sativa Cruz
Marilyn M. Cuneo*
Alice Daugherty
Kelly Davidson
Azima Davis
Linda Davis
Tami Davis*
Joyce G. Davison*
Abigaille de Mesa
Colleen Denney
Kelli DePuy*
Ruth DeRose
Stacey Devine
Patricia Dingleberry

Yolanda Dixon
Liz Dodson
Jessica Dorrance
Sarah Kathryn Dossett
Kelly Douglas
Rachelle Dowdy
Kamillah Drayton
Gianna Drogheo*
Beatrice Dulberg
Sandra D. Duncan*
Miya Dunham
Linda Durham*
Michelle Dussault
Lauren Duthie
Joan A. Dytman
Cynthia Eakes
Rachael Eastman
Dean Edgington
Lillie G. Edwards
Mary Jane Edwards
Melissa Elk
Sarah E. Ellis
Tiffany Ellis
Navine Elmasri
Maggie Ens
Camille Esposito
Tiffany Eubanks
Kareemah Evans
Naomi Extra
Bethany Fancher
Sarah Farmerie
Susan Farnham
Mary Faulkner
Alicia Faxon*
Loie Fecteau
Kathleen Ferguson
Katherine R. Fields*
Kimberly Fields
Michele Finkelstein
Diana Flanagan
Jill Foote-Hutton
Adrienne Ford
Jennifer Ford
Anne C. Fowler
Charlotte Fox
Joy Fox
Marjorie Franke
Trisha Franzen*

Kathy Freise*
Anna Fusco
Jan Gallaway
Alice Galvin
Sonya Garber
Debra Garcia y Griego*
Dawn Gardenhour
Elizabeth Garlington
Misc. Pippa Garner
France Garrido
Tara Garten
Cheronda Giles
Sandy Gillespie*
Danielle Glatt
Amy Golahny
Cecilia Griffin Golden
Ellen Golden
Jean Goldfarb
Barbara Goldstein*
Ruby Gómez
Africa Gonzales
Brisa Gonzales
Teresa Gonzalez
Anne Clair Goodman
Zola K. Gordy
Katherine Gore
Ilona Granet
Beth L. Gray
Frankie S. Gray
Aylin Green
Luella Margaret Greene
Elizabeth Grew
Barb Grossman
Sandra Groves
Kate Gubata
Christine Haas
Amanda Habel
Kim Hafner
Camille Hamilton
Patti Hammond-Kovach
Anne Hanley
Glenda L. Harris
Sterling Harris*
Veronica Harris
Shivaughn Hatt
Adrienne Haught
Terri Berthiaume
    Hawthorne

Amber Hellon
Laurie Hemler
Lauren Henderson
Donna Henes
Penny Henry
Savannah Esperanza
    Hernandez
Ioanna Georgiadou
    Hershberger
Andrea J. Heugatter
Laura C. Hewitt
Debra Higgins
Jill Hindenach
Brenda Hinshaw
Lois Ann Hobbs
Audrey Hollander
Bryant Holsenbeck
Azize Homer
Laurie Homer
Caroline Honour
Kaitlyn Horpedahl
Jane Howard
Jennifer Howison*
Kathy Hsieh
Megan Hucks
Crystal Huggins
Heather Hughes*
Sandi Hughes*
Carissa Hussong*
Grayson Maye Lusk Hussong
Barbara Hutchens
Colleen Hutchens
Yolanda Hvizdak
Jaime Hypes
Dana Jacobs
Laura A. James
Pat Clements Jaquay
Pamela Jennings
Antonia Jiminez
Mariasol Johannes
Ava R. Johnson
Jazzmone Johnson
Jess Sarah Johnson
Mary Jo Johnson
Nichica Johnson
Alice Johnston
Amelia M. Joiner
Jan Jones

Megan Jones
Anita Jung
Lyn Kartiganer
Julia E. Katz
Nita Kehoe Gadway*
Julie Kern
Angelle Khachadoorian
Halima Khan
Dwyer Kilcollin
Rachael King
Erma Hughes Kirkpatrick*
Courtnay Kittell
Rachel Kizielewicz
Katelin Conklin Kleissler
Risa Korris
Ottie L.
Chris L.
Racheallee Lacek
Corine Landrien
Mary Turner Lane
Anna Laurenzo
Carolyn Law
Isis Lawson
Maia Lazarus
Jennifer Leach
Deborah Lee
Gwen Left Hand Bull
LaVerne B. Lein
Beverly K. Lennen*
Debbie Lerner
Nerys W. Levy*
Takeesha Lewis
Carrie Lieb
Micaela Lindsey
Nicole D. Lopez
Susan M. Lopez
Carey Lovelace
Keren Lowell
Anna Marie Ludwig*
Amy Luick
Wendy Lyford
Anne Marie Lynch
Chenille J. Lynch
Shanice Mackey
Kerri Mader
Toni Malone
Devyn Manibo
Ethel Manibo

Erika Mann
Lee Marchalonis*
Margaret Marley*
Tamia Mathews
Julie Mattsson
Jennifer Mayer
La'Tasha D. Mayes
Alyce Mayo*
Julia Preston McAfee
Anne McCarroll
Tara A. McComb*
Carol L. McCoy
Judith McCoy
Kristin McDonough*
Yolanda McDowell
Teri McElhaney
Kathleen Cadeliña-Elgarico
    McElroy
Meg Anne McGurk*
Tasseli McKay
Rachel McKinney
LaSherrie McKinnie-Bates
Claudia McLean
Stowe McMurry
Anne McNaughton
Christine Merritte
Jessica H. Meyer
Sarah Michael
Jo Michalski*
Angela Mileschkowsky
Kathi Miller
Lauren M. Miller
Kelly Miller-Smart
Marchell Milley
Alexis Mitchell
Sarah Mitchell
elaine monbureau
Allison Moore
Margaret L. Moore
Rosa Moore
Joanne K. Morris
Tereneh Mosley
Janet B. Moss
Lorraine Mucha
Nile Mueller
Jalesse Munoz
Erin Murphy
Leola Nagitsy

Neeve
Neltje*
Rachelle Nesta
Judy Nethercott
Rebecca Newlin
Juliana M. Newton
Christiane Nickel
Ann Nimon
Liz Nysson
Denise Oberdan
A. Stephanie Oglesby
Lorraine O'Grady
Kate Okeson
Sherri Olsen
Susan Olson
Donna M. O'Neal
Leah Orejudos
Draga Orescanin
Gina Ortiz
Mary Owen
Connie Ozer
Natalie Padilla
Jean Parish*
Stephanie Parrish*
Katherine Patten
Sara Peller
Neisha Peoples
Thelma D. Perkins
Donna Petersen
Patricia Phair
Donna Marie Phillips
Stephanie Pierce
Rhonda B. Pope
Janey Potts
Joyce Presley*
Heidi Preston
Linda L. Pretz
Mary L. Pretz-Lawson*
Betsy Puckett
Margaret Quail
Kate Holbein Rademacher*
Julie Rafferty
Jasleen Rana
Ann Randolph
Carol Rardin
Tracy Rawlings
Lynn Reeves*
Sheryl Maree Reily

Caroline L. Reinhart
Polly Rhodes*
Arlene Rich
India Jessup Richards
Kathleen Richardson
Judy Riddell
Kyan K. Rios
Stephanie Rivera
Annie Rivers
Lydia Roberson
Peggy Robinson
Heide L. Rogers
Pennie Roland*
Jaquille Rollins
Adeola Roluga
Ann Roylance
Chloe Rubenstein
Tanya Taylor Rubinstein
Emily Rudnick
Dina Rudofsky
JS
Bipasana Sakya
Liesl Salameh
Jenny Sanborn
Anna B. Sandoval Girón
Annette Santamaria
Peggy Scales
Lee Schaffler
Lucy P. Schultze
Iris Scott
Mary Katherine Scott
Shaffe Scott
Wanda Seamster
Anna Sears
Beth Sellars
Carey-Taylor Seward
Priya Shah
Paula Shanks
Susan Share
Kelley Sharp
Shannon Flattery Sharp
Ann Davis Shaw
Sedra Sheikh
Uruj Sheikh
Elizabeth Shelley
Lateasha Shirer
Renna Short
Peggy Shumaker
Vaughn Sills

Wendy Simanton
Sofia Simons
Nannette E. Slingerland
Nikki Smerski
Adeline Josie Smith
Louise R. Smith
Stacey Sudduth Smith*
Laura Sonora
Mary Eileen Sorenson
Erika Soveranes
Dorchelle T. Spence
Harmony Dancing Rain
    Spoonhunter
Wilma Weed Spoonhunter
Cecile Springer*
Danielle W. Standish
Bertha Steptoe
Ev Stone
Rae Strother
Ruth B. Stroud
Caitlin Stroup
Julie Stunden
Alison L. Suggs
Jody Sunshine
Brandon Bain Sutton
Vivian Swallow
Wilma Swallow
Heather Swanson
Mariya Tarassishina
Suzanne Taugher
Jill McLean Taylor*
Maeve L. Taylor
Dawn C. Tedesco
Gail Terzuola
Robin Tewes
RoJean Thayer
Janine Thibedeau
SallyAnn Thibedeau
Robyn Thomas
Sallie Threlkeld-Wesaw
Marisa Tilenina
Crystal H. Todd
Cheryl Tolentino
Jay Tompkins
Diane Torr
Terri Trapp
Anne Trauben*
Andrea Trettel
Michele Troutman

Amy J. Trueblood
Natasha Trujillo
Cinna Turnbull*
Caitlin Denney Turnek
Ann Turner
Erin Tweed
Dora B. Urban
Monina Vanderveer
Aleide Van Zandweghe
Claudia Villareal
Suzanne Volmer
H.C. Arin Waddell
Kim Wade
Helen A. Waldorf
Allyson Walker
Dorothy Wanamaker
Leslie J. Warner-Sanders
Marguerite H. Watson
Hanae Weber
Jake Weber
Amy Weinmeister
Towana Welch
Stephanie Werthman
Garrett Ann Wexler
Launda Wheatley
Tevy Wheatley
Judy White
Valorie White
Ada R. Shane Whiteman
Bille Wickre*
Marty Williams*
Courtney Wilson
Frances Wilson
Martha Wilson*
Kara Winerman
Elyssa Winzeler
Elizabeth D. M. Wise*
Sherri Wood
Elly Worden
Rana Wright*
Rebecca Wurzburger
Colleen Wyse
Ruri Yampolsky
Claire A. Yannacone
Christina Yao
Emily Yates
Bonnie Zare
Susan Zirbel

About the Authors

Tiffany Ludwig is an artist and New Jersey native who currently lives in Glen Ridge. She received her BFA from the Mason Gross School of the Arts of Rutgers University.

Renee Piechocki is an artist who lives in Pittsburgh, Pennsylvania. She received her BA from Hunter College of the City University of New York.

Tiffany Ludwig and Renee Piechocki began their collaboration Two Girls Working in 2001. *Trappings* is their first project.